Understanding
World History

The History
of Slavery

Other titles in the series include:

Ancient Chinese Dynasties
Ancient Egypt
Ancient Greece
Ancient Rome
The Black Death
The Decade of the 2000s
The Digital Age
The Early Middle Ages
Elizabethan England
The Enlightenment
The Great Recession
The History of Rock and Roll
The Holocaust
The Industrial Revolution
The Late Middle Ages
The Making of the Atomic Bomb
Pearl Harbor
The Renaissance
The Rise of Islam
The Rise of the Nazis
Victorian England

Understanding
World History

The History
of Slavery

Hal Marcovitz

Bruno Leone
Series Consultant

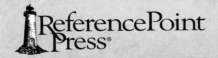

ReferencePoint
Press®

San Diego, CA

© 2015 ReferencePoint Press, Inc.
Printed in the United States

For more information, contact:
ReferencePoint Press, Inc.
PO Box 27779
San Diego, CA 92198
www.ReferencePointPress.com

LIBRARY OF CONGRESS CATALOGING-IN-PUBLICATION DATA

Marcovitz, Hal.
   The history of slavery / by Hal Marcovitz.
     pages cm.—(Understanding world history)
   Audience: Grade 9 to 12.
   Includes bibliographical references and index.
   ISBN 978-1-60152-742-4 (hardback)—ISBN 1-60152-742-X (hardback)
 1. Slavery—History--Juvenile literature. I. Title.
   HT861.M27   2015
   306.3'6209--dc23

                                                     2014010454

Contents

Foreword

When the Puritans first emigrated from England to America in 1630, they believed that their journey was blessed by a covenant between themselves and God. By the terms of that covenant they agreed to establish a community in the New World dedicated to what they believed was the true Christian faith. God, in turn, would reward their fidelity by making certain that they and their descendants would always experience his protection and enjoy material prosperity. Moreover, the Lord guaranteed that their land would be seen as a shining beacon—or in their words, a "city upon a hill"—that the rest of the world would view with admiration and respect. By embracing this notion that God could and would shower his favor and special blessings upon them, the Puritans were adopting the providential philosophy of history—meaning that history is the unfolding of a plan established or guided by a higher intelligence.

The concept of intercession by a divine power is only one of many explanations of the driving forces of world history. Historians and philosophers alike have subscribed to numerous other ideas. For example, the ancient Greeks and Romans argued that history is cyclical. Nations and civilizations, according to these ancients of the Western world, rise and fall in unpredictable cycles; the only certainty is that these cycles will persist throughout an endless future. The German historian Oswald Spengler (1880–1936) echoed the ancients to some degree in his controversial study *The Decline of the West*. Spengler asserted that all civilizations inevitably pass through stages comparable to the life span of a person: childhood, youth, adulthood, old age, and, eventually, death. As the title of his work implies, Western civilization is currently entering its final stage.

Joining those who see purpose and direction in history are thinkers who completely reject the idea of meaning or certainty. Rather, they reason that since there are far too many random and unseen factors at work on the earth, historians would be unwise to endorse historical predictability of any type. Warfare (both nuclear and conventional), plagues, earthquakes, tsunamis, meteor showers, and other catastrophic world-changing events have loomed large throughout history and prehistory. In his essay "A Free Man's Worship," philosopher and mathematician

Bertrand Russell (1872–1970) supported this argument, which many refer to as the nihilist or chaos theory of history. According to Russell, history follows no preordained path. Rather, the earth itself and all life on earth resulted from, as Russell describes it, an "accidental collocation of atoms." Based on this premise, he pessimistically concluded that all human achievement will eventually be "buried beneath the debris of a universe in ruins."

Whether history does or does not have an underlying purpose, historians, journalists, and countless others have nonetheless left behind a record of human activity tracing back nearly 6,000 years. From the dawn of the great ancient Near Eastern civilizations of Mesopotamia and Egypt to the modern economic and military behemoths China and the United States, humanity's deeds and misdeeds have been and continue to be monitored and recorded. The distinguished British scholar Arnold Toynbee (1889–1975), in his widely acclaimed twelve-volume work entitled *A Study of History*, studied twenty-one different civilizations that have passed through history's pages. He noted with certainty that others would follow.

In the final analysis, the academic and journalistic worlds mostly regard history as a record and explanation of past events. From a more practical perspective, history represents a sequence of building blocks—cultural, technological, military, and political—ready to be utilized and enhanced or maligned and perverted by the present. What that means is that all societies—whether advanced civilizations or preliterate tribal cultures—leave a legacy for succeeding generations to either embrace or disregard.

Recognizing the richness and fullness of history, the ReferencePoint Press Understanding World History series fosters an evaluation and interpretation of history and its influence on later generations. Each volume in the series approaches its subject chronologically and topically, with specific focus on nations, periods, or pivotal events. Primary and secondary source quotations are included, along with complete source notes and suggestions for further research.

Moreover, the series reflects the truism that the key to understanding the present frequently lies in the past. With that in mind, each series title concludes with a legacy chapter that highlights the bonds between past and present and, more important, demonstrates that world history is a continuum of peoples and ideas, sometimes hidden but there nonetheless, waiting to be discovered by those who choose to look.

Important Events in the History of Slavery

1750
Babylonian king Hammurabi issues the Code of Hammurabi, believed to be civilization's first set of written laws; the code institutionalizes slavery.

1095
The Crusades begin as Christian soldiers lay siege to the holy lands of the Middle East. For the next two centuries thousands of Christians and Muslims are captured and sold into slavery.

1562
English admiral John Hawkins captures three hundred Africans in Sierra Leone and sells them to a Spanish colony on the island of Hispaniola in the Caribbean, establishing Hawkins as the most successful slaver of the era.

1794
France abolishes slavery.

BCE   CE 1000   1200   1400   1600   1800

135–73
The three Servile Wars are fought between rebellious slaves and the Roman army. All three wars result in defeat for the slaves.

1619
The first African slaves arrive in the colony of Jamestown, Virginia.

1200s
Slavery begins to die out in Europe, replaced by the system of serfdom in which slaves are granted their freedoms but still made to live in hopeless poverty and perform labor for landowners.

1787
Colonial leaders draft the US Constitution in Philadelphia; the document includes the Three-Fifths Compromise, permitting slavery to remain legal in America but counting a slave as three-fifths of a citizen for purposes of deciding representation in Congress.

1381
The Peasants' Revolt erupts in England as serfs rebel against their poverty and servitude to wealthy landowners.

1857

The US Supreme Court issues the *Dred Scott* decision, finding that slaves are not American citizens and therefore have no constitutional rights.

2013

Fourteen Caribbean countries announce plans to seek reparations from the European nations that enslaved their citizens in past centuries.

1861

Czar Alexander II abolishes serfdom in Russia.

1865

The Confederacy surrenders on April 9, and on December 6 the Thirteenth Amendment to the US Constitution is adopted, abolishing slavery in America.

1850　　　**1900**　　　**1950**　　　**2000**

1948

The United Nations issues the Universal Declaration of Human Rights, outlawing all forms of slavery.

1863

Lincoln signs the Emancipation Proclamation, freeing all slaves in states rebelling against the Union. The slaves would not know true freedom for another two years, following the defeat of the Confederate army.

1939

World War II erupts in Europe and Asia; in Europe the Germans employ slave labor in munitions factories, while in Asia the Japanese turn two hundred thousand captive women into prostitutes.

1859

On October 16 Abolitionist John Brown stages a raid on the US military arsenal at Harpers Ferry, Virginia. Brown's plan to provoke an armed revolt against slavery fails, and he is hanged two months later.

The Defining Characteristics of Slavery

By the first century BCE, the population of the Roman Empire—which stretched across Europe, the Middle East, and North Africa—stood at roughly 1 million people. A third of those people were slaves.

Most Roman slaves had been citizens of lands conquered by Roman armies. They were taken into captivity and sold at slave auctions. As the property of their owners, they were forced to work on farm fields, in mines, or as laborers helping build new Roman cities. Many were household slaves, assigned to domestic chores. Trusted slaves were placed in charge of shops or other businesses. Regardless of the work they were assigned to do, though, there is no question that most slaves of ancient Rome seethed under the rule of their masters and hoped one day to escape servitude.

In fact, slave uprisings were common in Rome. It was not unusual for a slave to attack a master and attempt an escape—an infraction punishable by death. In 135 BCE a Roman slave named Eunus led a widespread uprising on the island of Sicily. As many as seventy thousand slaves joined the revolt, but three years later the Roman army vanquished Eunus's followers, ending what is known as the First Servile War. A similar uprising, known as the Second Servile War, erupted on Sicily in 104 BCE and again was cut down by the Roman army.

In 73 BCE Roman slaves revolted a third time. Unlike the first two conflicts, the Third Servile War was not limited to the island of Sicily. The conflict spread throughout the Italian peninsula of Europe as tens of thousands of slaves joined the revolt. For a time the uprising threatened to topple the government of Rome. The leader of the revolt was a gladiator—a slave expected to fight to the death in the arena for the entertainment of Romans. His name was Spartacus.

The story of Spartacus has entered popular culture because numerous books and films have been produced chronicling his saga. Certainly, though, Americans need not look to ancient Rome to learn lessons about slavery—the enslavement of people has been very much part of the story of human civilization since the ancient era.

The Institution of Slavery

Moreover, slavery has played a significant role in the history of the Americas. Starting in the sixteenth century, Africans were captured in their native lands and shipped across the Atlantic Ocean where they were forced to work in the Caribbean and later on the plantations of the American South. Slavery endured as an institution in America until the South was vanquished in the Civil War and, soon after the end of the war in 1865, the Thirteenth Amendment to the US Constitution was adopted.

One of the causes of the Civil War was the rise of the Abolitionist movement, which during the first half of the nineteenth century grew from a tiny yet vocal minority into a major political movement. Although many slaves were freed by the Emancipation Proclamation in 1863, most slaves would not know true freedom for another two years. That turning point arrived only after the South's top military leader, Robert E. Lee, surrendered to Union general Ulysses S. Grant, at Appomattox Court House in Virginia, ending the Civil War.

But as the story of Spartacus illustrates, slavery was an institution in human civilization for thousands of years before Grant accepted Lee's surrender. Slavery has been known on virtually every continent and, in fact, is still part of the human existence in many areas of the globe. It has often been institutionalized by law—the first known written

African slaves are forced aboard a ship bound for the Americas. Slavery in the American colonies began in the sixteenth century and lasted in the United States until the adoption of the Thirteenth Amendment to the Constitution in 1865.

constitution, the Code of Hammurabi, was composed in about 1750 BCE by the Babylonian king Hammurabi and included provisions for the treatment of slaves. Other bodies of laws, including the original US Constitution, have similarly addressed the status of slaves but stopped short of freeing the hapless individuals.

The main reason people seek to enslave others is economic: They require cheap labor to produce agricultural products or other goods, work as prostitutes or soldiers, or even perform household chores. Through the use of force or by employing their wealth, they are able to obtain slaves and maintain them in servitude. Says Jeremy Black, a historian at the University of Exeter in Great Britain, "The variety of slavery in the past and across history stretched from the galleys of Imperial Rome to slave craftsmen in Central Asian cities . . . and from the mines of the

New World to those working in spice plantations in East Africa. Public and private, governmental and free enterprise, slavery was a means of labour—and a form of control."[1]

Slavery has been denounced by individual governments as well as international organizations, including the United Nations. Since the era of ancient Rome, slaves have rebelled or have been freed after bloody conflicts. Over the course of history, perhaps millions of lives have been lost by those who have sought to free slaves as well as those who have fought to maintain the institution of slavery in their countries. And yet slavery remains part of modern life. In the course of world civilization, there has never been a time when humans have not sought to own other humans.

Chapter 1

What Conditions Led to Slavery?

For tens of thousands of years, slavery was unknown on the planet. The earliest humans—the hunter-gatherers—had no use for slaves. Their entire existence was devoted to finding food and shelter for themselves and their families or tribes. Throughout this age there was no agriculture, commerce, or accumulation of wealth and therefore no need for slaves. In fact, slaves would have been a burden to these people: slaves would have to be fed. Says historian Milton Meltzer, "Men were able to kill just enough game to feed themselves, and there was no surplus to feed captives."[2]

Only when civilizations began to take root would slavery become part of the human experience. Soldiers captured in battle were forced into slavery. Whole families were made into slaves if they had the misfortune of living in a city vanquished by an invading army. Survivors of shipwrecks were often sold into slavery. Kidnappings and piracies were common in the ancient era, and the victims often found themselves for sale at slave auctions.

Slavery was such an accepted part of human existence that virtually nobody—except perhaps the slaves—thought it was wrong. The Greek philosopher Aristotle—one of the most enlightened Western thinkers of the ancient age—regarded slaves as nothing more than property. In 350 BCE Aristotle wrote, "For the slave has nothing in common with his master; he is a living tool, just as a tool is an inanimate slave."[3] In fact, Aristotle added, a slave can expect no more out of life than work, food, and punishment.

A Symbol of Status

By the time Aristotle wrote those words, Greece had emerged in Western civilization as a society devoted to the sciences, arts, and literature. The Greeks were an agricultural people—their diets consisted largely of grains and fruits—and therefore they were dependent on farming. To bring in their crops, Greek farm owners used slave labor.

The Greeks were also builders. They erected elaborate stone temples to their gods. The largest of these temples was the Parthenon, built in the fifth century BCE in the city of Athens. The Parthenon was composed of 20,000 tons (18,144 metric tons) of white marble. Carved into the walls were illustrations depicting events in Greek history. Standing at the entrance to the Parthenon was a 40-foot (12 m) statue of the goddess Athena, after whom the city was named. It took more than twenty years to build the Parthenon. This tremendous example of Greek architecture, the remnants of which remain standing today, was built mostly with slave labor.

The Greeks used slaves for much more than hard labor; harvesting crops; or quarrying, cutting, and laying stone. For a free Greek man or woman, there were virtually no goods or services that were not provided by slaves. Says Meltzer, "Slaves milled grain, baked bread, sewed cloaks, mixed drugs, and concocted perfumes."[4]

Slaves were bought and sold in slave markets. Owning slaves was regarded as a symbol of status in Greek society. The wealthiest Greeks may have owned as many as fifty slaves. The master would not leave the house without slave attendants trailing behind. At home women slaves performed the household chores. Even free Greeks who were not wealthy often found the means to own at least one or two slaves. According to Meltzer, Greeks went into debt so they could own slaves, much as people in the modern world take on debt to obtain luxuries such as big houses or expensive cars that they cannot afford. "To the Greeks, slavery was necessary," says Meltzer. "Society could not go on without it, they believed. The aristocrat preferred to give his time and energy and intelligence to public affairs, the arts, recreation, and war. The forced labor of other men freed him from the manual labor of the . . . period and allowed him to pursue his higher interests."[5]

The Slaves of Chios

Perhaps in no place in ancient Greece was slavery more a part of life than on the island of Chios. (The island was then—and still is—under the dominion of Greece, but it can be found just a few miles off the Turkish mainland in the Aegean Sea.) By the fifth century BCE, thirty thousand free citizens lived on Chios, along with one hundred thousand slaves.

Slavery was vital to life on Chios because the island had emerged as a wine-making center in the ancient Greek world. As such, slaves were needed to provide cheap labor to the vineyard owners. Says Sara Forsdyke, professor of classical literature at the University of Michigan:

> The reason for the early and extensive use of slaves on Chios is to be found in its status as a relatively large and fertile island conveniently located to optimize on trade routes. Slave labor was the necessary ingredient to transform these natural endowments into wealth. By employing slaves on their lands, the Chians were able to produce surplus amounts of wine, figs, and other agricultural products that they then exported for profit.[6]

Prisoners of war are sold as slaves in ancient Greece. Slave ownership was considered a symbol of status in Greek society.

Chios serves as one of history's first examples of how slavery grew into a vital component of the local economy. Indeed, the vineyard owners of ancient Chios needed the slaves to tend and harvest their grape crops and work in the wine-making trades. Without the steady supply of cheap labor, Chios would not have been able to produce the grapes and wine that made the free citizens of the island wealthy. This form of slavery can be found throughout history, perhaps most notably in the pre–Civil War American South, where plantation owners determined they could not raise cotton at a profit without the use of slave labor.

Slavery was so important to life on Chios that the island emerged as the slave-trading capital of ancient Greece. On Chios slaves were sold to buyers who came from as far away as Persia—modern-day Iran—in search of cheap labor.

Moreover, Chios was also the site of one of history's first slave uprisings. In the sixth century BCE, a slave named Drimachus led other slaves in revolt. He led his followers into the mountains, where they easily held the strategic upper hand against armies sent to root them out. Eventually, the Greeks gave up. Drimachus often led raids into the Chios lowlands, freeing slaves and butchering slave owners who were known to be cruel. For centuries after his death, Greek slaves worshipped Drimachus, believing him to be a god who watched over them.

Government Slaves

In ancient Greece even the government owned slaves. During this era Greece was not a united nation but rather a loose federation of city-states whose citizens shared a common language, traditions, and deities. Some city-states, such as Athens and Sparta, were large and required cheap labor to maintain streets, government buildings, parks, and other public places. Slaves were also used as clerks, jailers, and even as executioners. So it was not unusual to find government officials at slave auctions making bids for slaves alongside private buyers.

In Athens even the police force was composed of slaves. In the fourth century BCE, the Athenian army captured three hundred archers in

How True Is the Story of Moses?

Anybody who has sat through Sunday school has undoubtedly heard the story of Moses. According to religious teachings, Moses led the Jewish people out of slavery in Egypt and, after wandering in the desert for forty years, brought them to their homeland—today the modern state of Israel. According to the Bible, Moses was born a Jew but raised as an Egyptian prince. As royalty, he once saw a taskmaster abusing a Hebrew slave, and Moses came to the slave's defense by killing the Egyptian master. He was forced to flee Egypt but returned as a messiah, determined to lead the Jewish people out of slavery.

Scripture assigns many miracles to the story—that Moses, through the hand of God, brought down ten plagues on the Egyptians to convince their leader, the pharaoh, to release the Jews from slavery. Also, as he led the Jews out of Egypt, Moses is said to have commanded the Red Sea to part so the Jews could escape from an Egyptian army.

Scholars believe there is at least some truth to the story of Moses and the Exodus of the Jews from Egypt sometime between the sixteenth and thirteenth centuries BCE. Says historian Will Durant, "The story of the 'bondage' in Egypt, of the use of the Jews as slaves in great construction enterprises, their rebellion and escape—or emigration—to Asia, has many internal signs of essential truth, mingled, of course, with supernatural interpolations customary in all the historical writing of the ancient East. Even the story of Moses must not be rejected offhand."

Will Durant, *Our Oriental Heritage: The Story of Civilization*, vol 1. New York: Simon & Schuster, 1954, p. 301.

Scythia, a region of Central Asia where the nation of Kazakhstan can now be found. Taken back to Athens, the Scythians were put to work by the local government in the city-state's police force. "They were armed and had the power to arrest free men,"[7] says Meltzer.

Athens is regarded as the home of democracy. In the sixth century BCE, the Athenian ruler Cleisthenes instituted a system of governance in which all citizens were given a voice in the administration of the city-state. Athenian citizens met on a hillside, where they debated issues and cast votes on matters of governance. A few citizens were elected to hold offices in the military and oversee the treasury. In fact, the word *democracy* finds its roots in the Greek words *demos*, which means "people," and *kratos*, which means "power." Of course, slaves had no rights to cast votes on that Athenian hillside. "Slavery, however, had been part of Greek life for centuries, and the emerging belief in democracy and freedom did not challenge it,"[8] Meltzer writes.

No Hope of Winning Their Freedom

Still, the slaves owned by the Athenian government were well treated in many respects. They were allowed to live in their own homes and provided money on which to live. They could earn tips. They were permitted to marry and raise children. They were permitted to own personal possessions such as furniture. Otherwise, though, the slaves enjoyed no other benefits of Greek citizenship: the right to own their own businesses, defend themselves in court, and of course, return to their homelands. They were, after all, still slaves.

In fact, slaves owned by the city-state governments had virtually no hope of winning their freedom. In Athens and other city-states, government officials turned over so many important duties to the slaves that the officials knew full well without the slaves their governments would be unable to operate. Free citizens often agreed to serve their governments as elected officials for brief periods, but most were anxious to return to their private lives. The slaves, on the other hand, would always be there and always know how things were meant to be done. "Elected officials came and went in short terms, but the public slave stayed on the job," says Meltzer. "He knew tradition and form; he knew what worked and what did not. He became indispensable to the officials above him."[9]

Relentless Work and Servitude

Although the slaves owned by the Greek governments as well as by most private owners knew no hope of winning their freedom, some fortunate slaves were freed by their masters. In the fourth century BCE, a slave named Pasion was bought in the slave market by two bankers, Antisthenes and Archestratus, who entrusted him with clerical duties. Pasion became so valuable to the business that his two masters granted him his freedom and eventually turned the bank over to him. Pasion became a very wealthy man—and the owner of many slaves. In fact, when Pasion died he left the bank under the guidance of a slave named Phormio, who eventually gained his freedom as well.

But stories like those of Pasion and Phormio were rare in the ancient Greek world. For most slaves life consisted of relentless work and servitude. To defy one's master meant punishment, often by flogging. Indeed, one aspect of life in ancient Athens that annoyed free citizens was the fact that, on a busy street in Athens, it was impossible to tell the slaves from the citizens. Custom demanded the slave step aside to permit a free citizen the right of way, but few did; how was the citizen to know a slave, and not another freeborn citizen, was blocking his or her way? Under the law a free citizen could strike a slave without fear of reproach, but the unprovoked striking of a fellow citizen could result in arrest and punishment.

The fourth-century-BCE Athenian statesman Demosthenes told the story of how he received a complaint from a citizen whose slaves were assaulted by a group of drunken adolescents. Evidently, smoke from a cooking fire ignited by the slaves had drifted over to where the youths were drinking. Annoyed by the smoke, the youths assaulted the slaves—even defecating on them. Robert Osborne, professor of ancient history at King's College in Cambridge, England, asserts, "One has a picture of a society where, when citizens could recognize slaves, some of them were prepared to treat them to routine and unprovoked abuse, and where the only source of restraint was the fear of turning out to have so treated someone whose body was protected by the law. . . . Torture, beating, branding, whipping and hard labour left their marks written on the slave body."[10]

Slavery in the Roman Empire

For the slaves of ancient Greece, life could be fraught with abuse, endless labor, and physical punishment, but for the free citizens of Greece, ordinary life was often filled with danger as well. During the ancient era the city-states were often at war with one another, a circumstance that made the country vulnerable to foreign invaders. During the second century BCE, many of the Greek city-states fell under siege by Roman invaders. Greek citizens captured by the Romans found themselves serving in slavery.

Rome replaced Greece as the preeminent society of Western civilization. The Romans also believed in democracy and took democratic governance a step further than the Greeks, establishing an elected senate to

The Roman army faces a Carthaginian force during the Second Punic War. Tens of thousands of Carthaginians were captured and sold into slavery.

pass laws and administer the government. Under the Roman republic, citizens were granted human rights and representation in their government—but such benefits were not enjoyed by slaves. Indeed, in Rome slaves were no better off than they had been in Greece. One early Roman leader, Dionysius I, who ruled around 400 BCE, was known to sell the entire populations of captured cities into slavery.

During the Punic Wars of the second and third centuries BCE, in which Roman armies fought against the North African empire known as Carthage, tens of thousands of Carthaginians were captured and sold into slavery. In 63 BCE Rome conquered Judea; some one hundred thousand Jews were sold into slavery. In 58 BCE the Roman general and first emperor, Julius Caesar, took more than fifty thousand prisoners when he conquered Gaul—a region that today encompasses France and Belgium. He sold them all as slaves.

The Slave Auctions

The conquerors who enslaved their enemies turned the profits of the slave sales over to the Roman government, making Rome the wealthiest society in the ancient world—certainly, a reason Rome dominated much of Europe, the Middle East, and North Africa for more than five hundred years.

In 509 BCE a popular uprising against a despotic ruler led to the establishment of the Roman republic. Romans elected senators to govern and make laws. For citizens of Rome human rights were guaranteed under a set of laws known as the Twelve Tables. For slaves the institution of the republic and creation of the Twelve Tables provided no relief. In fact, the Twelve Tables institutionalized slavery. Under the Twelve Tables a free citizen convicted of the crime of theft could be sentenced to slavery; a slave convicted of theft could be put to death.

Every city in the Roman Empire had its slave market, where traders auctioned the captives to bidders. Some cities actually had slave emporiums—where shoppers could find the laborers they needed on any given day. More commonly, though, auctions were held in public squares or markets on specific days. Meltzer writes:

The usual method of sale was the auction. The place might be the town's cattle market, an open area crowded with animals, buyers and sellers. At one end a space would be cleared, and the auction block set up. The slave dealers would march their wares by gangs—men, women, and children, usually of many races and nationalities. The crier would mount the block and bark out the announcement of the sale. As the buyers drew near, the auctioneer would mount the block, motion the slave to step up on a raised platform, and the sale would begin.[11]

Buyers were free to approach the slave and prod or feel the slave's body. Some of the buyers bought slaves specifically to teach them household skills or crafts, then resold them at a profit. Cato the Elder, the second-century-BCE orator and statesman, made himself rich by buying slaves and reselling them as trained workers.

As in Greece, Roman slaves were expected to perform household chores as well as heavy labor in the fields or the mines or in building Roman cities. There were some cultural differences: In ancient Greece, household slaves were sold for lower prices than manual laborers, but in Rome, where fine dining had been elevated to an art, an expert cook could command a high price at the slave auction. Wealthy Romans educated their slaves and entrusted them with running their businesses—Romans regarded commerce as work that was beneath them and readily turned the sordid chores of running their shops over to their slaves. Virtually all Roman entertainers—actors, singers, and musicians—were slaves. And as the story of Spartacus illustrates, slaves were trained as gladiators and sent into the arenas to fight, and die, for the entertainment of audiences.

Rebellious and Vengeful

Spartacus was a native of Thrace, a region of ancient Greece that today is part of Greece, Turkey, and Bulgaria. How Spartacus became a slave is unknown—the most popular myth suggests he was captured by the Roman army. By 73 BCE, the first year of the Third Servile War, Spartacus had been sold to the Roman Lentulus Batiates, who operated a school

Slavery and the Code of Hammurabi

Slavery was institutionalized as far back as the eighteenth century BCE when King Hammurabi, ruler of the city-state of Babylon—a region in what is now Iraq—composed what is believed to be the first written body of laws. Although the Code of Hammurabi is regarded as a sincere attempt by the king to ensure all his subjects were treated equally under law, the code dictated by the king nevertheless ensured that slavery remained a way of life in Babylon.

The Code of Hammurabi did not outlaw slavery; instead, the code established a series of rules spelling out how slaves were to be treated by their masters and other free citizens. For example, if a citizen was found guilty of blinding or breaking the bones of another citizen's slave, the offending citizen could be forced to pay the slave's master half the value of the injured slave. A free citizen found to be harboring a runaway slave could face the death penalty. A slave who defied a master could have his or her ears cut off.

However, under the code, slaves did have some rights. Masters were not permitted to kill their slaves. Also, family members sold into slavery by husbands or fathers to satisfy debts were automatically freed after three years of servitude.

for gladiators in the city of Capua. Conditions at the school were harsh, and the fates of the students were all but assured—virtually all gladiators died in the arenas. The students at the school rebelled, and seventy-three managed to escape, seeking shelter in the countryside. They chose Spartacus as their leader. The Roman historian Plutarch heaps praise on Spartacus, describing him as "a man not only of high spirit and bravery but also in understanding and gentleness superior to his condition."[12]

As word of the slave uprising in Capua spread, many slaves escaped from their masters to join Spartacus. Eventually, Spartacus found himself at the head of a slave army that numbered some 120,000 members. Spartacus's original plan was to march the slaves north into the Alps, where the army would disperse so the freed slaves could make their way to their homes. However, many members of his slave army were rebellious and vengeful—they aimed to make the Romans pay for their harsh treatment in servitude. As the army made its way north, many members of the slave army conducted raids into towns, looting and killing.

Alarmed by the violent behavior of the slaves, the Roman Senate dispatched an army to put down the uprising. Battles between the slaves and the Roman soldiers raged for months. Finally, the slave army's march to the north was halted by a superior force of Roman soldiers. Unable to continue north, Spartacus turned his army south with the intention of attacking Rome. The senate reconvened and, recognizing the revolt as a true threat to the existence of Roman society, mustered new troops to confront Spartacus. As the Roman army advanced, Spartacus realized he could not take the city of Rome. Instead, he decided to lead the army past Rome to the southern coast of Italy, where he hoped his army could escape by commandeering ships and sailing to Africa.

The final confrontation occurred in 71 BCE at the Battle of Siler River in the far southern portion of Italy. The slaves fought bravely— Spartacus was killed in the battle, but not before taking the lives of two Roman commanders. The six thousand slaves who survived the battle were taken captive and crucified along the Appian Way, a road that leads to Rome. Says historian Will Durant, "Their rotting bodies were left to hang for months, so that all masters might take comfort, and all slaves take heed."[13]

Value and Entitlement

Although Spartacus and his slave army suffered a devastating defeat, it was not unheard of for slaves to win their freedom. In ancient Greece Drimachus won his freedom with the sword, whereas Pasion and Phormio won their freedom by making themselves invaluable to their masters' businesses. And there are surely some examples of slaves who managed to slip away and, through their guile and resourcefulness, find their way back to their homelands. But such cases are believed rare in the ancient world.

Even an army of some 120,000 slaves led by Spartacus could not fight its way to freedom in ancient Rome. The wealthy and powerful aristocrats of ancient Greece and Rome knew the value of slaves—without slavery, it is doubtful whether the vineyard owners of Chios would have attained their wealth and status as the best winemakers in ancient Greece. Slavery was vital to the way of life in the ancient world, and the free citizens of Greece and Rome, despite their devotion to democratic principles, still saw the value and entitlement in owning their fellow humans.

Chapter 2

Slaves of the Medieval Era

By the tenth century CE, the Germanic tribes of central Europe were regularly attacking towns in Poland, Russia, and the Baltic states. The towns were looted and burned, and their citizens were rounded up and sold into slavery. A major slave market emerged in the cities along the coast of the Adriatic Sea in a region known as Dalmatia, which today is part of the nation of Croatia. The victims of this slave trade were the Slavic peoples of Europe. In fact, so many Slavs were sold into slavery during the medieval era that *Slav* is regarded as the root of the word *slave*.

But Slavs were not the only peoples enslaved during the Middle Ages. Following the fall of the Roman Empire in the year 410 CE, slavery remained part of human civilization throughout Europe, the Middle East, and Asia. In the eighth century the Vikings attacked England and took their captives back to the Norse countries as slaves. The Vikings called their slaves "thralls." (The original meaning of the word *enthralled*—which today means "to be in awe"—was "to be enslaved.") Starting in the eleventh century, Christian soldiers known as crusaders traveled to the Middle East to retake the holy land from Islamic potentates. If they were captured in battle, the Christians found themselves facing a lifetime of slavery.

In feudal Japan, China, and other Asian lands, vanquished peoples knew very well they would live the remainder of their lives as the properties of their captors. "During the early Middle Ages, slavery was a common state of life," claims historian and author Ruth A. Johnston. "Slavery was not racial; it was the result of conquest. When a city was captured, its women and children were usually taken or sold as slaves, and its men were also pressed into hard slavery in mines or on ships, if they were not killed."[14]

Era of Feudalism

The medieval era endured from the fifth century through the fifteenth century. In Europe and other lands, it was an era of warfare, lawlessness, and the reign of feudal rulers who maintained their authority through their wealth and brute force. As in ancient Rome or Greece, slaves were expected to provide labor for their masters. Europe was largely an agrarian society during the medieval period, so most slaves were sent to work in the fields. In tenth-century England, a clergyman named Bishop Aelfric recorded the words of a field slave:

> I go out at dawn driving the oxen to the field and yoke them to the plough. It is never so harsh a winter that I dare lurk at home for fear of my master, but when the oxen have been yoked and the ploughshare and coulter fastened to the plough, I must plough each day a full acre or more. . . . I must fill the oxen's manger with hay, and water them, and clear out the dung. . . . It is heavy work, because I am not free.[15]

In England it is likely that the slave who told his story to Bishop Aelfric found himself in servitude due to an unpaid debt or the commission of a crime. If men were married when they were forced into slavery, their wives were given permission to remarry. Runaway slaves were put to death if captured, usually by stoning. If they managed to escape, English slaves often made their way to other countries, where they hoped to find wage-paying work and save to repay their debts so they could one day return to their homeland.

Under the German rulers known as the Franks, the plight of slaves could be particularly harsh. Frankish slaves were often brutally beaten—one Frankish noble, Duke Rauching, is known to have extinguished his candles by pressing them against the flesh of his slaves.

A Viking warrior sells a slave girl to a Persian merchant. The Vikings sold some of their captives and brought others back to the Norse countries as slaves.

Cruel Treatment of Slaves

Rauching was not a unique practitioner of cruelty when it came to the treatment of slaves during the medieval era. Throughout history the plight of the slave had always been one of servitude and toil; nevertheless, some earlier civilizations had taken steps to protect slaves from excessive cruelty. During the reign of the pharaohs, who ruled Egypt from about 3,000 BCE to 30 BCE, masters who raped their slaves could be sentenced to as many as one thousand lashes. Certainly, slaves were the properties of their masters and otherwise had no rights under Egyptian law; nevertheless, Egyptian judges also believed slaves had no way of defending themselves and therefore looked harshly on owners who took such liberties with their slaves.

By the Middle Ages, though, such legal protections were rare. As such, slave owners had virtually unbridled power to treat their slaves with the harshest of measures. For example, the branding of slaves became common in the Middle Ages—owners ordered hot irons pressed into the skin of their slaves, burning painful and permanent marks of ownership into their bodies. The hot irons were often pressed into cheeks or foreheads. Moreover, the unfortunate slave who was sold to a new owner would likely have to endure a second branding as his or her new owner sought to place proof of ownership onto the slave's body. "This was one of the many brutalities inflicted on slaves," insists Mark T. Gustafason, professor of classical studies at Calvin College in Michigan. "Others included whipping, beating, shackling, dismemberment, and mutilation."[16]

In the Norse countries it was not unusual for Viking kings to maintain harems of forty or more slave girls. When a king died, one unfortunate girl was taken out of the harem and slain. As part of the Viking funeral ritual, the slave girl's body was burned in the pyre along with the body of her master.

Slavery During the Crusades

As cruel as conditions may have been for slaves in Europe, the unfortunate souls who found themselves enslaved in the Middle East could hope for no fairer treatment under their Islamic captors. From 1095 through 1291, Christian armies from Europe laid siege to Jerusalem and other Middle Eastern cities during a series of wars known as the Crusades. These European armies hoped to oust Islamic regimes and restore their dominion over the holy lands of the Middle East.

Many of the knights and princes who led the sieges regarded the Crusades as much more than a religious mission: They traveled to the Middle East with the intention of plundering the vanquished cities of the Arab world. In addition to the gold and other treasures seized by the Europeans, tens of thousands of captured Muslim men, women, and children were rounded up and shipped back to European slave markets. During his travels, the twelfth-century Arab poet Ibn Jubayr made this observation: "Among the misfortunes that one who visits their land will see are the Muslim prisoners walking in shackles and put to painful labour like slaves. In like condition are the Muslim women prisoners, their legs in iron rings. Hearts are rent for them, but compassion avails them nothing."[17]

The Children's Crusades

One of the saddest chapters in the history of the Middle Ages occurred in 1212 when a twelve-year-old shepherd boy named Stephen from the village of Cloyes in France led a crusade to retake the holy land. At the time, the Christian armies had suffered numerous defeats, but Stephen believed his mission was blessed by God. He convinced thirty thousand children to follow him to the Middle East.

The children made their way to the city of Marseilles on the Mediterranean coast, where they boarded seven ships. Years later a priest returned from a tour of North Africa and claimed to have encountered some of Stephen's followers. They were now adults, the priest reported, and all were slaves. Evidently, the children who boarded the ships had been duped by the captains into believing they would be delivered to the Middle East where they could continue their crusade. Instead, the unscrupulous captains sold them into slavery.

A second Children's Crusade, led by a German boy named Nicholas, also took place in 1212. Some twenty thousand children attempted to make their way to Rome, where they intended to ask for the blessing of Pope Innocent III before continuing their crusade. Although some children died during the march, many made it to Rome, where Innocent advised them to turn back. Most of the children heeded the pope's advice and returned to their homes, although many certainly died on the return journey. Some children are believed to have boarded a ship bound for the Middle East. Their fates remain unknown.

But it was the Muslim armies that ultimately prevailed during the Crusades. Thousands of Christian soldiers who followed their princes to the Middle East never returned—many were slain in battle, to be sure, but tens of thousands were captured and enslaved. The Battle of Hattin, for example, resulted in a crushing victory for a Muslim army under the leadership of the sultan Saladin. The battle occurred in 1187 in what is today the nation of Israel. The Christian army, under the leadership of a Frankish noble, Guy of Lusignan, had been lured into an open field by Saladin, whose superior force overwhelmed the Christian army of some twenty thousand soldiers.

Following the battle, thousands of Guy's men were sold into slavery. (Guy escaped slavery—he was ransomed and permitted to return home.) In fact, the Franks captured during the battle were so numerous that when they flooded the slave markets of the Middle East, frustrated traders found prices dropping due to the overabundance of available slaves. Says Yvonne Friedman, professor of history at Bar-Ilan University in Israel, "Saladin's secretary stated that there were so many captives in Muslim hands after the Battle of Hattin that their price deteriorated on the slave market and a man could be bought for a pair of sandals."[18]

The Life of a Eunuch

By the 15th century the center of the slave trade in the Islamic world was Istanbul, located in modern-day Turkey. The Koran—the holy book of the Islamic people—forbids the enslavement of Muslims. As such, the slaves sold in the markets of Istanbul as well as other cities in the Middle East or North Africa were likely to have been soldiers or other Europeans captured during the Crusades. Africans and Asians captured in conflicts or kidnapped from ransacked towns were also forced into servitude.

As in Europe, the slaves of the Middle East were used in the fields or for other laborious tasks but were also valued by wealthy aristocrats and potentates for household services. Among the most unfortunate of the slaves were the eunuchs—castrated men who were assigned to various household chores, most notably guarding the harems (which were, invariably, composed of slave girls) of potentates and other wealthy Muslims.

Typically, young boys captured in vanquished cities were castrated before they reached puberty. If they survived the mutilations of their

Armies clash in a bloody battle during the First Crusade. Captives of both Christian crusaders and Muslim warriors endured a cruel fate; many were enslaved for the remainder of their lives.

genitals—excessive blood loss and infections were common and medical care was rudimentary, at best—the eunuchs faced dismal lifetimes of servitude. Under Islamic law, castration of Muslims was forbidden, and so most eunuchs were Slavs, Greeks, Indians, or Africans.

In addition to ensuring that the eunuch would pose no threat to the sultan's harem, castration was regarded as a method of ensuring the slave's loyalty. By making certain the slave would never father children, the only family a eunuch would know would be the family of his owner. Therefore, the eunuch was expected to regard himself as a member of the ruler's family and give his full loyalties to carrying out the wishes of his master.

Some eunuchs were entrusted with significant responsibilities that went beyond guarding harems. They became valued members of the palace household and forged close bonds with the wives of the sultans, helping raise the sultan's children. "When an inordinately young or mentally deficient prince gained the throne, his mother and the chief eunuch could find themselves virtually running the empire,"[19] asserts Ohio State University historian Jane Hathaway.

Nevertheless, regardless of how they may have endeared themselves to their masters, the eunuchs were still slaves. They were never permitted to buy their freedom nor were they otherwise granted freedom by their owners. If a eunuch was permitted to own any property at all, upon his death that property was seized by his master.

Serfdom in Europe

By the fifteenth century much of the Middle East and North Africa had been conquered by the Ottoman Empire, a sultanate based in Istanbul. The Ottomans condoned the ownership and trade of slaves well into the nineteenth century. But in Europe slavery began to fade almost seven hundred years earlier. The feudal landowners of the era had not found softer hearts; rather, the cause of the decline in European slavery was due to the changing economic climate. Through warfare or debts owed by landowners, their large estates were being broken up into smaller tracts—as such, large stables of slaves to tend the fields were unnecessary and costly. Moreover, landowners found that slaves facing lifetimes in bondage were far less willing to work than if they were granted a measure of freedom. And so the system of serfdom emerged throughout Europe. The term *serf* finds its roots in the Latin word *servus*. Will Durant contends, "It was the serf, not the slave, who made the bread of the medieval world."[20]

In reality, however, the life of the serf was hardly an improvement

The Vikings who captured their enemies often took them back to the Scandinavian countries as slaves. But unlike most slaves of the medieval era, the Viking slaves, known as thralls, often did not face hard labor. At the time agriculture was not widely practiced in the Norse countries. Therefore, thralls served mostly as symbols of status and wealth for their Viking masters.

Young women were often turned into concubines, but others were given little else but household chores to perform. Historian Milton Meltzer explains, "They served no important function within Scandinavia. The land had no workshops and no plantations or great manors that needed slave power. The thralls became household servants, desired chiefly to put up a noble's prestige."

Eventually, the Vikings found they could trade their thralls for goods. Starting in the seventh century, the Vikings set up trading posts in western Russia. The Russians needed slaves to work on their farms, and they were willing to trade furs, wax, and hides for them. Some Vikings sailed as far east as Constantinople, the Turkish city later known as Istanbul, where they found traders willing to exchange silks, spices, and fruits for thralls.

Milton Meltzer, *Slavery: A World History*, vol. 1. Cambridge, MA: Da Capo, 1993, p. 220.

over the life of a slave. The landowners ensured that even serfs they had freed would owe a lifetime of debt to the owners. Moreover, the terms of serfdom ensured that a serf's descendants remained in debt to the landowner as well. A serf was required to remain on the land, pay rent, and turn over a portion of his crops and earnings to the landowner. Indebted to the landowner, the serf forever toiled for this new form of master.

Moreover, in some countries the serf was still considered the property of the master. In France the law permitted landowners to sell their serfs, or the labor of their serfs, to other landowners. Throughout Europe a landowner held the power to round up all his serfs and assign them to labors such as digging canals, clearing woodlands, or building dikes. If a baron needed to raise an army, his serfs were obligated to serve. Jeremy Black writes, "Serfs could be bought and sold, and families could be split up and moved against their wish."[21] Serfdom in Russia was probably the cruelest form: The laws did not protect serfs, meaning that if a serf was accused of a crime, the landowner decided the punishment. Flogging was typical retribution.

Unbearable taxes were common during this era as well, further keeping serfs impoverished. It was the rare serf who found the means to break away from the grip of the landowner. Says Black, "Serfdom entailed restrictions on personal freedom that, in their severe form, were akin to slavery, and it has been argued that many aspects of medieval serfdom were very like slavery. . . . Serfs were subject to a variety of obligations, principally labour services, and owed dues on a variety of occasions, including marriage and death."[22]

The Peasants' Revolt

The slaves of ancient Rome rebelled three times and, during the Third Servile War, threatened the government of Rome itself. But the serfs of Europe, at least initially, accepted their circumstances. Many held their barons in high regard, considering themselves fortunate to be given their freedom—even if that freedom included a lifetime of debt and backbreaking labor. A reason for their acceptance of serfdom could be found in their lord's responsibility to protect them from thieves, marauders, and enemy armies. If an invader successfully took the baron's land, the lives of his serfs were not necessarily guaranteed.

A serf family lived in a cottage that was just a step above a shack. Typically made of twigs with a straw roof, the cottage usually featured just a single room. Inside, a fireplace provided heat. The cottage featured rough-hewn furniture, an earthen floor, and a single mattress shared by everyone—husband, wife, and children. "Pigs and fowl had the run of the house," says Durant. "The women kept the place as clean as circumstances would permit, but the busy peasants found cleanliness a nuisance, and stories told how Satan excluded serfs from hell because he could not bear their smell."[23]

By the fourteenth century, however, serfs were far less amenable to the whims of their masters. During the 1340s, the plague known as the Black Death wiped out huge populations in Europe. Many of those who died were serfs. "Not surprisingly, the greatest number of victims came from the poor," Milton Meltzer states. "Ill-cared for, sick, hungry, they were least able to resist sudden death."[24] The serfs who survived demanded change. The Peasants' Revolt erupted in England in May 1381 when tax collectors tried to collect new taxes on all citizens, including serfs. At the time, England was at war with France and the government needed taxes to maintain its army. In the town of Kent, the serfs rioted and drove off the tax collectors. Similar riots spread through other English towns. On June 11 rebels from across England formed a mob and

Serfs work the land under the watchful eyes of an overseer. Serfdom was little better than slavery; as property, serfs could be bought and sold at the whim of the landowners.

marched on London. The rebels entered London on June 13 and were welcomed by Londoners who were also hostile toward the new tax. Riots broke out throughout London—one place that was ransacked was the Temple, a district in London where the city's lawyers kept their offices. The serfs harbored ill feelings toward London lawyers because the lawyers had written the deeds of servitude that kept them impoverished and in serfdom while their masters reaped the rewards for their labors.

The Landowners Prevail

On June 15 the fourteen-year-old English king, Richard II, agreed to meet with the rebel leader Wat Tyler. During the meeting the lord mayor of London, William Walworth, believed Tyler to be acting rudely toward the young king and struck Tyler with a sword. One of the king's bodyguards then finished the job, plunging his sword into the rebel leader. Hundreds of rebels witnessed the killing and, raising their bows, advanced toward the king and his guards. At that point, Richard stepped forward to calm the rebels. "Sirs, will you shoot your king?" he asked. "I will be your chief and captain; you shall have from me that which you seek."[25]

To meet their demands the young king agreed to abolish serfdom in England. The rebels returned to their homes believing they had achieved their aims, but they soon learned they had been duped. Instead of granting their freedom from serfdom, Richard dispatched his troops into the countryside to arrest the rebellion's leaders. Later Richard met with a delegation from Essex that asked him to render his promise of June 15 into written form. The king refused. "Villeins you are still, and villeins you shall remain,"[26] he declared. (*Villein* is another term for *serf*.)

Eventually, more than one hundred leaders of the Peasants' Revolt were arrested and executed. That fall the English Parliament took up the question of freeing the serfs. The members of Parliament, who were virtually all landowners, voted to maintain the system of serfdom. Says Durant, "The beaten peasants returned to their plows, the sullen workers to their looms."[27]

The End of Serfdom

The Peasants' Revolt may have been put down, but not since the Third Servile War had a regime been so threatened by an uprising of the enslaved. For decades after the failure of the Peasants' Revolt, the serfs made it clear they were unhappy with the heavy taxes and feudal rules that kept them in servitude. British historian Michael Wood writes:

> On the face of it, the rising of 1381 appears to have achieved nothing. So why is it a turning point? It did not lead to a statute abolishing serfdom but it did lead lords to take the safer course and, instead of farming their . . . lands with unwilling servile labour, they leased their lands and lived on the rents rather than the produce. In this way, villein tenure (land held in return for compulsory labour services) disappeared.[28]

Indeed, the serfs were eventually freed from servitude not by an act of revolution but by a gradual change in the economic conditions of England as well as other European nations. For centuries serfs had been required to provide labor and turn over portions of their crops to the landowners, but as the Middle Ages ended, the exchange of currency became more common. As such, serfs came to be regarded more as tenant farmers who paid rents to their landowners than as virtual slaves required to provide labor. John Kellis Ingram, historian at Trinity College in Ireland, says, "The relation of owner and occupier came to be regarded as a result of a contract. Serfdom died out in England without any special legislation against it."[29]

Finally, in 1574 Queen Elizabeth I freed the last remaining serfs. Over the next three hundred years, serfdom was wiped out in other countries as well. The French Revolution of 1789 provided the French people with many human rights, including freedom from serfdom. In Russia, Czar Alexander II freed the serfs in 1861. Throughout Germany, Spain, and other European countries, rulers were forced to put down the occasional uprising, and by the latter years of the nineteenth century, serfdom had gradually been eliminated throughout the European continent.

Over the course of the Middle Ages, an era covering some one thousand years, slavery and later serfdom remained part of human civilization. As in the ancient era, people could find themselves enslaved through all manner of circumstances: They may have been soldiers captured in battle or families living in towns vanquished by marauding barbarians. However they may have found themselves in the throes of slavery, these unfortunate souls had to endure cruelties seemingly invented specifically to make their lives unbearable. The slave girls sacrificed as part of the Viking funeral rite, the young boys suffering castration in the Middle East sultanates, the slaves burned for Duke Rauching's pleasure, and the serfs duped by Richard II's false promises were all victims of one of slavery's most brutal eras.

Chapter 3

Slavery in the New World

By the 1500s the West African kingdoms of Ndongo and Kongo—regions of what are the modern-day nations of Angola and Congo—had been conquered by Portugal. African slaves were much valued, and during the first century of Portuguese conquest, thousands were captured. Some remained in Africa, working in salt or tar mines. Many slaves, though, were shipped to other countries—mostly in the Middle East, because by then slavery in Europe had long been replaced by serfdom, and even serfdom was dying out.

If the slaves left Africa, it is likely they were loaded onto ships in the port city of Luanda, which today serves as Angola's capital. In 1619 about 350 African slaves were herded onto a Portuguese ship in Luanda. Soon after the ship embarked on its voyage, it was attacked by two British pirate vessels that seized between forty and sixty slaves. The pirates sailed west across the Atlantic Ocean. They were aware that a dozen years earlier, more than one hundred English citizens had established a colony in the New World in Jamestown, Virginia. Although by 1619 the colony had grown to a population of some one thousand, the pirates knew conditions were often harsh in Jamestown—the colonists were struggling to make the settlement a success, particularly in the farm fields. The pirates suspected the colonists may be in the market for some slaves.

After several weeks at sea, the pirate ships arrived in Jamestown—probably in August. They traded some of the Africans for food, then left Virginia and sailed for Bermuda, where they found buyers for more slaves. A few months later the pirates returned to Virginia, sold the final nine or ten slaves to the Jamestown colonists, and left the New World. In all, between twenty and thirty African slaves are believed to have arrived in Jamestown in 1619. Williamsburg, Virginia, historian James Horn says, "Few could have seen the momentous consequences"[30] of that initial transaction.

England's Slave Ships

The arrival of slaves in Jamestown marked the beginning of what is regarded as the darkest chapter in American history. Over the next 246 years, more than 4 million people were enslaved in America. However, decades before the slaves were sold to the Jamestown farmers, African slaves had already been toiling in South America, Central America, the Caribbean islands, and even on North American soil. In fact, the Portuguese slave ship attacked by the British pirates was heading for Veracruz in Mexico when it lost some of its cargo to the privateers.

By the reign of Queen Elizabeth I, the English had established a healthy commerce with Spanish traders in Brazil and the West Indies, where they obtained textiles, gold, pepper, and other goods. In 1562 a British navy admiral, John Hawkins, arrived at the coast of Sierra Leone in West Africa, where he captured three hundred Africans. Hawkins transported his cargo to a Spanish colony on the island of Hispaniola—today the home of the nations of Haiti and the Dominican Republic—where he traded the slaves for animal hides, ginger, sugar, and pearls.

When Elizabeth heard of the admiral's venture, she was at first outraged—she opposed slavery—but when she learned of Hawkins's profits, the queen changed her thinking. In fact, in 1564 the queen invested her own money in Hawkins's second slaving voyage. In that venture Hawkins obtained hundreds of slaves in Sierra Leone and sold them in Venezuela.

As Hawkins became the most successful slaver of the mid-sixteenth century, he found willing partners among the kings of African tribes. Forever at war with one another, the African kings were anxious to rid themselves of their enemies, so they were delighted to sell their captives to Hawkins—who would soon be joined by other English slavers as

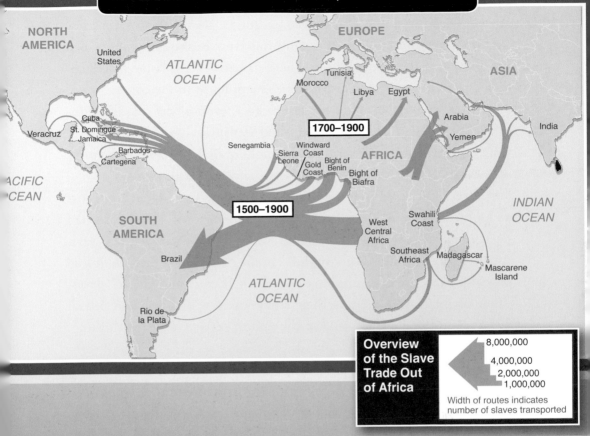

American Slave Trade, 1500–1900

NORTH AMERICA

United States

ATLANTIC OCEAN

EUROPE

Tunisia

Morocco

Libya   Egypt

ASIA

Arabia

India

Cuba
St. Domingue
Veracruz   Jamaica

Barbados

Cartegena

Senegambia   Windward Coast

Sierra Leone / Gold Coast   Bight of Benin

AFRICA

Yemen

1700–1900

Bight of Biafra

PACIFIC OCEAN

SOUTH AMERICA

1500–1900

West Central Africa

Swahili Coast

INDIAN OCEAN

Brazil

Southeast Africa   Madagascar

Mascarene Island

ATLANTIC OCEAN

Rio de la Plata

Overview of the Slave Trade Out of Africa

8,000,000
4,000,000
2,000,000
1,000,000

Width of routes indicates number of slaves transported

well as those from Portugal, Spain, and France, in selling African slaves to buyers in the New World. In 1672 England's King Charles II granted a charter to the Royal African Company; headquartered in Liverpool, by 1800 the company was sending 120 ships a year to the African coast to buy slaves, who were then sold in America.

Indentured Servants

English entrepreneurs may have found robust profits in selling slaves to American farmers, but it was Spanish slavers who introduced the slave trade in the New World. In 1528—nearly a century before the establishment of the Jamestown colony—a Spaniard, Lucas Vasquez de

43

Ayllon, arrived in Virginia to establish a colony. He was accompanied by five hundred Spanish colonists—and one hundred African slaves. Fever struck the colony, which also endured a slave revolt. After a few months de Ayllon and his surviving followers broke camp and sailed for Haiti. In 1565 a Spanish settlement named St. Augustine was established in Florida. Again, slave labor was employed in the colony.

By the time slaves arrived in Jamestown, most of the colony's arduous labor was performed by indentured servants, colonials whose lives were only marginally better than those of slaves. In return for the price of passage or to satisfy other debts, many new residents of Jamestown—and, later, other colonies—agreed to terms of servitude that could last as long as fourteen years. Some indentured servants, those who had been convicted of crimes in England, often found themselves in servitude for life. Milton Meltzer writes, "In the New World the indentured servants lived under conditions not much better than chattel slaves. They got no pay in wages. Their compensation was bed and board, a chance to learn a trade, and at the end of service, perhaps clothing, tools, or grant of government land. The master set the hours and working conditions and determined the punishments for disobedience."[31]

As with the institution of serfdom, indentured servitude would also die out. As the colonies grew in population and commerce between Europe and America increased, the price of passage fell to the point that many people could make the crossing without going into debt. Moreover, when American cities such as Boston, New York, and Philadelphia grew and life became much more cosmopolitan than in the earliest days of the colonies, many Europeans of means were drawn to America, bringing their wealth along with them.

Slavery South of the Border

However, in the jungles of Central and South America and the Caribbean islands, the cosmopolitan life found in Boston, Philadelphia, and New York was unknown. Slaves were needed to work on the vast sugar plantations or harvest bananas and the other agricultural products found in the tropics. These countries were under the dominion

Slave Breeding

As a concession to Abolitionists in Congress, the southern states agreed to a voluntary ban on the importation of slaves in 1808. The ban meant that all slaves had to be native born. To maintain a steady supply of slaves for plantation work, many owners took steps to ensure that slave women would constantly be pregnant. In 1856 one slave owner boasted to the writer Frederick Law Olmsted that every slave baby was worth $200 to him. Wrote Olmsted:

> I hear the traffic spoken of incidentally, that the cash value of a slave for sale, above the cost of raising it from infancy to the age at which it commands the highest price, is generally considered among the surest elements of a planter's wealth. . . . A slave woman is commonly esteemed least for her laboring qualities, most for those qualities which give value to a brood-mare is, also, constantly made apparent.

> Male slaves were ordered to impregnate girls as young as thirteen, and by the time they were twenty-one female slaves were expected to have delivered a half dozen babies. As a reward for their talents as breeders, some slave women were given less work and better clothes.

Frederick Law Olmsted, *A Journey in the Seaboard Slave States*. New York: Dix and Edwards, 1856, p. 55.

of European powers. The first conquerors of these lands enslaved the native populations of Incas, Mayas, and Aztecs. In fact, by the time the Portuguese and Spanish conquistadors arrived in the sixteenth century, slavery was already a way of life in these regions. For generations these peoples had no qualms about enslaving rivals captured in warfare.

So as the conquistadors defeated the native populations, they enslaved their members and put them to work on farms and plantations. Sugar became a particularly valuable crop—the number of sugar plantations in Brazil alone grew from 30 in 1576 to more than 120 by 1625. Eventually, though, it would not be the native populations who toiled as slaves on these plantations but mostly Africans. Soon after the arrival of the conquistadors, Spanish and Portuguese priests made their way to the New World and set about converting the native peoples to Catholicism. By then the Catholic Church had established rules against enslaving Christians, which meant the plantation owners had to grant freedom to the indigenous peoples who accepted Christianity. So the plantations of Central America, South America, and the Caribbean islands turned to the African slave trade to fill their need for cheap labor.

The Revolutions of Simón Bolívar

Eventually, though, even the African slaves working on the tropical plantations would gain their freedom. Influenced by the desire for human rights voiced by the intellectuals of the European Enlightenment, the European countries started outlawing slavery by the late 1700s. By 1820 England, Denmark, Netherlands, Portugal, Sweden, Spain, and France had all outlawed the slave trade. By 1830 slavery had been outlawed in the colonies of Venezuela, Guatemala, Argentina, Peru, Chile, Bolivia, Paraguay, and Mexico.

Throughout South America the liberation of slaves can be attributed to the work of Simón Bolívar, who led revolutions in the early 1800s to free Ecuador, Colombia, Venezuela, Peru, and Bolivia from Spanish domination. Bolívar, a member of a wealthy slaveholding family, was nevertheless a dedicated abolitionist.

In some cases slaves were able to win their freedom through revolution: In 1801 the slaves revolted in the French colony of Saint-Domingue. Haiti, the new nation established by the freed slaves, immediately outlawed slavery.

Three-Fifths Compromise

Though European powers embraced the fall of slavery, the practice continued in America well into the nineteenth century. There were antislavery advocates active in the early colonial period in North America, but even after the new nation won its independence in 1783, they failed to bring about an overthrow of slavery. Southern agrarian society was deeply dependent on slave labor, and representatives from those colonies did not wish to cripple their economic advantages. During the Constitutional Convention of 1787, the interests of slaveholders were preserved to keep the fragile nation united. Antislavery delegates knew that if they pressed the issue, they would lose the southern delegates and the convention would end in failure.

With no federal constitution holding the loose union of states together, many delegates feared the British could exploit the divisions and return to reclaim their colonies. Believing they had little choice, the abolitionists in attendance at the Constitutional Convention dropped their demands for slavery to be outlawed in the new US Constitution. Instead, the only concession they managed to win from the slaveholding states was the agreement that for purposes of determining representation in Congress, a slave would not be counted as a full citizen but rather as three-fifths of a citizen. The southern delegates had demanded slaves be counted as full citizens, thereby giving them more members in the House of Representatives, whose membership is based on population. They settled, however, for the so-called Three-Fifths Compromise, an act that would not be repealed until after the Civil War.

As the Constitutional Convention adjourned, many of the antislavery delegates returned to their home states bitter over the Three-Fifths Compromise as well as their failure to outlaw slavery in America. One of those delegates was Benjamin Franklin, the printer, inventor, and statesman. In 1787, shortly after the end of the Constitutional Convention, Franklin ascended to the presidency of the Society for Promoting the Abolition of Slavery and the Relief of Negroes Unlawfully Held in Bondage—one of the first Abolitionist organizations in the country. In 1790 Franklin wrote to Congress, calling for the elimination of slavery:

"Mankind are all formed by the same Almighty Being, alike the objects of his care, and equally designed for the enjoyment of happiness."[32] James Jackson, a member of Congress from Georgia, dismissed the plea by declaring, "Let us hear no more of this detestable Proposition."[33]

King Cotton

Despite the steadfast support for slavery exhibited by the southern delegates at the Constitutional Convention, some historians believe slavery in America would have eventually died out on its own, because by the late eighteenth century many of the plantations and farms of the South were suffering through unprofitable years. The late 1700s saw a decline in the tobacco crop. Since the establishment of the Jamestown colony, tobacco had been the primary cash crop grown in the South. But the tobacco farmers of the era knew little about soil science: Years of tobacco farming had robbed their soils of the rich nutrients needed to grow bumper crops. They tried other crops but found little profit in rice, corn, and indigo or in growing mulberry fruit trees. Some tried raising silkworms to produce silk thread, but the production of silk is a complicated process that few farmers were able to master. Given that profits were so lean, many planters looked at the costs of buying and feeding slaves as too expensive. Historian Gavin Weightman says, "The old colonial slave economy was disappearing, a decline clearly signaled by the rapid fall in the price paid for slaves at the markets."[34] Indeed, in 1790 a healthy male slave could be obtained at an American auction for roughly the value of two years' worth of wages paid to a free farmhand.

The price of a slave would soon rise. In the latter years of the eighteenth century, as tobacco and other crops failed to provide much profit, few southern farmers saw the value in cotton. To harvest the crop and make it ready for spinning into thread, the seeds had to be separated from the cotton by hand. It was a laborious process, and few farmers found a way to make a profit by growing cotton.

That changed when a Massachusetts man, Eli Whitney, arrived at a Georgia plantation to begin a job as a tutor. In 1793, soon after his

Slaves use a cotton gin to separate the seeds from the cotton. Plantation owners turned to slave traders for cheap, plentiful laborers as cotton grew into one of the largest and most lucrative crops in the American South.

arrival, Whitney devised a machine to "gin" cotton. The device invented by Whitney—the cotton gin—used wire hooks to pull cotton through screens, mechanically separating the seeds. Soon after introducing the gin to southern farmers, Whitney boasted that a single machine could clear seeds from as much cotton in one day as one hundred field workers could accomplish. Practically overnight, Whitney transformed the South into the world's top cotton producer. In 1795 the American cotton crop yielded 8 million pounds (3.6 million kg); a decade later southern cotton growers were producing some 80 million pounds (36 million kg) per year.

Of course, now these growers needed vast numbers of workers to pick cotton, and to fill that need they turned to the slave traders. "The Yankee schoolteacher's gin that made cotton planters rich also made millions of black men and women slaves,"[35] contends Meltzer. Moreover, the planters' knowledge of soil science had still not advanced—cotton, like tobacco, robbed the soil of its nutrients. But cotton was too valuable a crop to stop production for several seasons to give the soil a chance to naturally replenish its nutrients. As a result, planters found new places to grow their crop—pushing the cotton belt west as far as Texas. As cotton growing moved westward, so did slavery. This increased emphasis on the cotton crop meant planters would need an abundant source of cheap labor; as such, by 1810 the price of a slave at auction was twice as much as it had been in 1790.

Plantation Life

Though millions of Africans had been imported to deal with cash crops in the South, most southerners did not own slaves. By 1860, of the 1.5 million free families in the southern states, fewer than four hundred thousand owned slaves. The South was largely rural during this era, and most people farmed small tracts of land and were too poor to own slaves. Only the large plantation owners could afford slaves, and even then, most used only a handful of field hands. About half the slave-owning families in the pre–Civil War era owned fewer than five slaves.

The wealthiest of the plantation owners numbered about ten thousand—these were the families identified in folklore as living in sprawling mansions that sat atop plantations comprising thousands of acres of cotton fields. Even so, of these ten thousand plantation owners, only about a third was wealthy enough to own one hundred or more slaves.

Regardless of whether they toiled on the largest of plantations or on the more modest farms of the era, field slaves typically lived in cabins on the owner's estate that were no better than the shacks occupied by the serfs in medieval Europe. The cabins had dirt floors and were heated with fireplaces; some were built of logs, but many were slapped together with slats of scrap wood. Cracks were filled with rags. Mattresses were stuffed with rags, straw, or grass. Blankets were rare luxuries.

The *Amistad* Rebellion

For African slaves the trip across the Atlantic Ocean was made in the dark, dank hold of a ship, chained together and packed shoulder to shoulder. In 1839 thirty-nine slaves aboard the slave ship *Amistad* escaped from their shackles, then found a supply of knives packed away in the hold. Arming themselves, the slaves waited until dark, then made their way to the deck, where they killed several sleeping crew members and took others captive.

The surviving crew members agreed to the slaves' demands to turn the ship back to Africa. At the time of the rebellion, the *Amistad* was sailing in the Caribbean Sea. Unknown to the slaves, the crew members did not sail back to Africa but zigzagged their way north. For seven weeks the *Amistad* rode the waves. Food and water ran short. At this point the *Amistad* was nowhere near Africa but instead off the coast of Long Island, New York. By now the Africans concluded they had been duped. They ordered the ship to land on the eastern tip of Long Island.

A US Navy ship caught up to the *Amistad* and took the slaves into custody, imprisoning them in New Haven, Connecticut. While the slave owners demanded their return, the slaves' cause was taken up by Abolitionists. In court the Africans were represented by former president John Quincy Adams, who argued the Africans' enslavement violated the US ban on the slave trade. In 1841 the US Supreme Court ruled the slaves had been illegally transported and ordered them freed. A year later, thirty-five survivors were given passage back to their homes in Africa.

The typical slave cabin measured about 256 square feet (23.8 sq. m)—about the size of a bedroom found in a modern-day house. As many as a dozen slaves—men, women, and children—lived in the cabin. Typically, a corner of a plantation was set aside for the slave cabins, all erected in a line or circle. Men and women worked in the fields, and usually by age five children were sent to work in the fields as well—to carry water or run errands. By age eight children were expected to pick cotton. The plantation slaves wore rags and ate meals of cornmeal, salted fish, and pork.

Slaves adopted the Christian religion and married, but weddings were rarely performed by ministers. Instead, a master typically declared a man and woman husband and wife. Families lived together but were often broken up. Slaves were frequently bought and sold among plantation owners, meaning fathers or mothers were taken away from their families. Even children could be taken out of their parents' arms and sold to new owners.

In fact, slaves rarely found opportunities to establish true family lives. The father was not the sole source of authority in the slave's family, as was common in most other families of the era; rather, the master set the rules for a slave's family. Says Meltzer, "Where plantation life became settled and a patriarchal master ruled the domain, slave families might develop some degree of permanence. But the stability of the family could always be broken by the will of the master. He could make or break the black family."[36]

Endless Toil

Life on a southern plantation was invariably one of endless toil that began with sunrise and ended after sunset, when it was too dark to see the cotton. Indeed, during the times of a bright full moon, the slaves were expected to stay in the fields well after darkness had fallen because the moon provided enough light to work. The only break the slaves received during the day was fifteen minutes or so at noon to eat the meager rations of cold bacon provided as their lunch.

As hard as slaves may have worked in the fields, if the masters thought they were slackers they could expect to be punished. One slave, Solomon Northrup, describes the typical punishments meted out to slaves:

When a new hand, one unaccustomed to the business, is sent for the first time into the field, he is whipped up smartly, and made for that day to pick as fast as he can possibly. At night it is weighed, so that his capability to pick cotton is known. He must bring in the same weight each night following. If it falls short, it is considered evidence that he has been laggard, and a greater or lesser number of lashes is the penalty.[37]

Raid on Harpers Ferry

As slaves endured these conditions, the Abolitionist movement continued to grow and find political support in many corners of American society. In the years leading up to the Civil War, Abolitionist leaders included William Lloyd Garrison of Massachusetts, who published the Abolitionist newspaper the *Liberator*; and Harriet Beecher Stowe, whose 1852 novel and play *Uncle Tom's Cabin* helped alert Americans to the cruel conditions under which slaves were forced to live. Meanwhile, slave revolts were common—the most notorious was the 1831 rebellion led by the slave Nat Turner, whose uprising on a South Carolina plantation took the lives of more than sixty white southerners. In retaliation, the South Carolina militia captured and killed dozens of the escaped slaves, including Turner, who was hanged.

By 1860, the eve of the Civil War, slavery had been abolished in eighteen of the thirty-three states. Over the years, the Abolitionists had hoped to convince Congress and the American people to outlaw slavery through peaceful and lawful means. Former slaves such as Frederick Douglass provided important voices to the movement as well. Meanwhile, the Underground Railroad was established by the movement to help escaped slaves make their way to the free states. But proslavery forces in Washington refused to concede the issue, pressuring Congress to pass the Fugitive Slave Act in 1850, which required runaway slaves to be returned to their owners. And in 1857 the *Dred Scott* decision by the US Supreme Court helped to further institutionalize slavery in the country. Dred Scott was a slave who sued for his freedom, claiming that he had been taken by his master to a state where slavery was illegal. But the Supreme Court ruled against Scott, finding that as a slave, he was not an American citizen and therefore enjoyed no rights under the US Constitution.

Abolitionists lead escaped slaves to freedom along the Underground Railroad. Abolitionists tried to convince Congress to outlaw slavery, but their efforts faltered.

Eventually, more radical leaders joined the Abolitionist movement. Among them was John Brown, who staged an armed raid on a US Army arsenal at Harpers Ferry, Virginia, on October 16, 1859. Brown and about twenty followers, including two runaway slaves, attacked the arsenal with the intention of obtaining arms to help build a force of armed Abolitionists. The army quickly responded to the raid and easily overpowered Brown and his followers. Brown was captured, convicted of treason, and sent to the gallows. On the morning of his execution on December 2, 1859, he handed the hangman a note that read, "I, John Brown, am now quite certain that the crimes of this guilty land will never be purged away but with blood."[38]

The End of Slavery in America

In 1860 Abraham Lincoln was elected president. During his campaign Lincoln opposed expansion of slavery into US territories. Lincoln's election and his inauguration on March 4, 1861, sent a signal to the slave states that they could no longer coexist with the free states. Even before Lincoln's inauguration, seven slave states announced their intention to secede from the Union and form the Confederate States of America, declaring they could not endure the presidency of a man they considered to be an Abolitionist. On April 12, 1861, Confederate soldiers fired on Union forces at Fort Sumter in South Carolina, touching off the Civil War. Another four slave states soon joined the Confederacy. The ensuing conflict cost the lives of more than six hundred thousand Americans. Outmanned, underfunded, and with little industrial base with which to build arms, the Southern states were finally forced to surrender in 1865. In December 1865 a reunited nation ratified the Thirteenth Amendment to the US Constitution, outlawing slavery.

For a time, slavery had found a home in the New World, where it remained an institution in the United States as well as the nations south of the border for decades after slavery was outlawed in Europe. The Europeans had discovered that slavery no longer suited their changing economies. Moreover, most of Europe embraced the ideas espoused during the Enlightenment, finding that slavery was morally wrong. But in North America and South America, slavery remained a vital component of their respective economies, making it advantageous for the wealthy and powerful to overlook the moral questions surrounding slavery. Plantations where valuable crops such as sugar, bananas, and cotton were grown required a source of cheap labor. These crops were so valuable that the owners of the plantations were willing to go to war to protect their way of life, even if war meant their countries were torn apart and hundreds of thousands of lives lost in battle.

Chapter 4

Slavery in the Modern Era

Visit any high school gym or city playground in America and chances are many of the young players are wearing Nike basketball shoes. Over the years, thanks largely to the endorsement of NBA legend Michael Jordan, the Nike brand—recognized by the company's familiar swoosh logo—has become one of the premier athletic shoes in America.

But in 2009 Nike customers learned a troubling fact about their shoes: Many were manufactured with cotton picked by slave laborers—including children—in the Central Asian country of Uzbekistan. When the facts about Nike's cotton supply surfaced, human rights groups—including British-based Anti-Slavery International—called for an international boycott of Nike products. Company officials were quick to react: In a statement, they insisted that they did not buy cotton directly from Uzbekistan but rather from independent importers and therefore did not know that slave-picked cotton entered the company's supply chain.

Nike pledged to investigate the sources of its cotton and cut ties with suppliers obtaining cotton from Uzbekistan. "Nike takes very seriously reports of widespread use of forced child labor in Uzbekistan cotton production," the company said in a statement. "We do not knowingly source cotton from Uzbekistan."[39]

The situation in Uzbekistan illustrates that well into the twenty-first century, slavery continues to be an institution that is promoted and accepted in many places on earth. And the fact that consumers in America and other industrialized countries may unknowingly buy products made with slave labor suggests that slave owners certainly have reasons to continue using the cheapest labor they can find—the labor of slaves.

Forced to Work in the Cotton Fields

Uzbekistan is one of the wealthiest nations in Central Asia. The former Soviet republic is a source of gold, uranium, and natural gas. The country is also a major supplier of cotton to world markets, exporting 3.3 million tons (3 million metric tons) a year.

In Uzbekistan private farmers own the cotton fields, but the government collects virtually all the profits from the cotton crop because officials have placed heavy taxes and other fees on farmers that ensure they remain in debt to the government. Each year the government of President Islam Karimov—regarded as one of the most despotic leaders in the world—forces 1 million Uzbeks to work during the cotton harvest. Many of the workers are children. They are given either the most minimal of wages—no more than a dollar a day—or, in most cases, no wages at all. During harvest time, workers are rounded up by the military and forced to live in squalid barracks near the cotton fields.

Workers cope with a massive pile of cotton. Hundreds of thousands of workers, including many children, are forced to work in the cotton fields of Uzbekistan for little or no wages.

made to work in brothels for the pleasure of Japanese soldiers. One Filipino woman, Maria Rosa Henson, recalled years later what life was like as an *ianfu*—a "comfort woman," or sex slave.

According to Henson, she was taken out of her home at age fifteen and made to live in a brothel, where she provided sex to twenty or more Japanese soldiers a day. Starting at two o'clock in the afternoon, the soldiers lined up outside her room. She says:

> We began the day with breakfast, after which we swept and cleaned our rooms. Then we went to the bathroom downstairs to wash the only dress we had and to bathe. The bathroom did not even have a door, so the soldiers watched us. We were all naked, and they laughed at us.

> When the soldiers raped me, I felt like a pig. Sometimes they tied up my right leg with a waistband or belt and hung it to a nail in the wall as they violated me. I was angry all the time.[42]

Occasionally, she said, the Japanese army sent a physician to the brothel to test the women for sexually transmitted diseases. Invariably, after making the tests, the doctor raped the women as well.

Preying on Young Women

Forcing women into prostitution is still part of modern-day slavery. Human traffickers are known to prey on young women from eastern European countries such as Moldova or Ukraine who, desperate to escape the poverty of their homelands, respond to job offers seeking waitresses or housekeepers in other countries. When the women arrive in these countries—often Israel, Germany, Switzerland, Japan, and the United States—they are forced to work as prostitutes. Typically, the employment agents in their own countries who arrange for their trips abroad are part of human trafficking networks that trap these women. When they arrive at their destinations, they are physically assaulted, raped, terrorized, and put to work in houses of prostitution.

One such victim was a young woman named Victoria who, at age seventeen, thought she was escaping the poverty of Moldova when someone she trusted told her about a factory hiring workers in Turkey. "There was no work, no money,"[43] she says of life in her country. The friend offered to drive her to Romania, where she could find transportation to Turkey; instead, the friend turned out to be a member of a human trafficking network who drove the girl to Serbia. Upon arrival, she was raped by Serbian traffickers and made to work in a brothel. Over the next two years, brothel owners bought and sold the girl several times, paying as much as $1,500 for her. Finally, she escaped and found shelter with a human rights group in the neighboring nation of Bosnia.

A prostitute from eastern Europe waits for customers on a street in the French city of Nice. Human traffickers promise foreign jobs to young, desperate women and then force them to work as prostitutes once they reach their destinations.

United Nations Resolutions

The slave traders who kidnapped Victoria, as well as the government of Uzbekistan, are engaging in conduct that is in violation of two United Nations (UN) resolutions. Those resolutions include the UN's Universal Declaration of Human Rights, adopted in 1948, which abolishes slavery in broad terms, stating, "No one shall be held in slavery or servitude; slavery and slave trade shall be prohibited in all their forms."[44] The second resolution, adopted eight years later, abolishes specific forms of modern slavery, including debt bondage, serfdom, forced marriage, and exploitation of children. And yet, according to the UN, as many as 21 million people endure slavery in the twenty-first century.

Uzbekistan joined the United Nations in 1992, but by 2014 the organization had taken little action to punish Uzbekistan for its promotion of slavery. A 2006 resolution to condemn Uzbekistan's record on human rights was blocked on the floor of the UN by the country's allies. Indeed, human rights activists have long complained that since adopting its antislavery resolutions, the UN has taken few steps to address modern-day slavery.

As in the case of Uzbekistan, allies frequently vote in blocs, preventing resolutions condemning particular countries from reaching the floor. "Many corrupt governments that retain good standing in the United Nations do little to combat human trafficking, a violation of natural rights against humanity,"[45] says Ericka Anderson, a political commentator for the Washington, DC–based public policy group the Heritage Foundation.

Slavery Today

Prostitution and forced farm labor are only two of the ways in which slavery remains part of human civilization in the twenty-first century. According to Kevin Bales, a former professor at Roehampton University in Great Britain, and Becky Cornell, a former staff member for the US Congress who specialized in antislavery measures:

> Although many people think slavery is a thing of the past, it exists all around us. In the rich countries of the world, slaves

suffer as servants, agricultural workers and prostitutes. In the developing world, slaves cultivate and harvest food, and work in small factories, the fishing industry and thousands of other jobs. Some of the commodities and goods they produce flow through the global market into our homes.[46]

According to Anti-Slavery International, slavery in the modern world often takes many forms. As in Victoria's case, human trafficking is a form of modern slavery. But women—and men—are trafficked for purposes other than sex work. Typically, when people arrive in a new country the traffickers take away their passports, denying them many rights. Without their passports, they cannot prove they have a right to be in the host country, and therefore they do not seek help from authorities. If they do, it is likely they will be deported back to their home countries. Without their passports, they are made to work in jobs for no pay. Factories, hotels, and farms are typically places where immigrant workers have been enslaved.

Another form of slavery found in the modern world is forced labor. The cotton field workers of Uzbekistan serve as an example. In some cases private employers in need of cheap workers will pay governments for the use of labor provided by prison inmates. The plight of child soldiers is known in many developing countries, particularly in Africa. In many armed conflicts children are sold into military service or kidnapped by commanders. They are handed weapons, given little training, and sent into the field to fight. Says Susan Tiefenbrun, a professor at Thomas Jefferson School of Law in San Diego, California, "The prevalent use of children in armed combat is a contemporary manifestation of slavery and a form of human trafficking that is as serious and as lucrative as the international crimes of trafficking in weapons and drugs. . . . Trafficking in children for their use on the battlefield is a human rights violation that rises to the level of slavery."[47] Enslaved children are often abused in other ways—made to work in farm fields, as beggars who turn over their alms to their masters, as household servants, or for sexual purposes.

Societies still exist in which the children of slaves are forced into

Child soldiers ride through the streets of Monrovia in the West African country of Liberia. In many armed conflicts in Africa, children are sold or kidnapped and forced into military service.

slavery—a form of slavery known as descent-based slavery. Anti-Slavery International says descent-based slavery is common in the West African nations of Niger, Mauritania, and Mali, where the caste system still exists. In such systems position in society is based on ethnicity, inherited wealth, tribal membership, and other factors. Those in the lower castes are often owned by members of the higher castes, and so are their children.

Bonded labor has been identified as a modern form of slavery. Bonded laborers are those who owe debts and are forced into slavery to repay those debts. Although it could be argued their wages go toward repaying their debts, that is rarely the case. Bonded laborers are prohibited from working for others to repay their debts; moreover, their masters typically make them work long hours, seven days a week, to repay debts that never seem to go away. "The value of their work becomes invariably greater than the original sum of money borrowed," says a statement by Anti-Slavery International. "Often the debts are passed on to next generations."[48] Places where bonded labor is common are Africa, Southeast Asia, and India.

In domestic slavery, women are typically enslaved, but men find themselves duped into domestic slavery as well. Many times wealthy people convince destitute people from other countries to live with them, promising jobs. But when the victims arrive, they are forced to work in their masters' households without pay. Again, the masters take the passports so the workers cannot prove to authorities they are in the country legally. That is what happened to a young woman named Matul, a seventeen-year-old from Indonesia who was promised a paying job as a housekeeper for a Los Angeles family. When she arrived, though, Matul was forced to surrender her passport and made to work without pay for two years. Her master, Matul said, "was threatening me, saying that if I ran away the police would arrest me because I didn't have my passport, and that I'd be thrown in jail where I'd be raped."[49] Matul was rescued by a human rights group, Coalition to Abolish Slavery and Trafficking, after a neighbor became suspicious and asked the group to investigate. The neighbor brought Matul to a shelter run by the coalition; she spent fifteen months there, earning a high school equivalency diploma and finding a legitimate job with a salary. Matul now rents an apartment with a roommate in the Los Angeles area. As for her former masters, they were never prosecuted; police lacked evidence to bring a case against them.

Slavery Investigations Are Rare

In Matul's case it took the efforts of a suspicious neighbor and a human rights group to uncover the case and spirit the victim away from her abusers. In many cases it has taken the efforts of human rights groups to identify victims of slavery, because few law enforcement agencies devote their resources to investigating slavery. Write Bales and Cornell:

> One of the most important areas needing resources is the training of police. In almost every country today, only the smallest number of police have been trained to identify slavery and trafficking and to use the most effective ways to investigate these crimes. Police officers often mistakenly view human trafficking victims as illegal aliens or criminals themselves. Governments need to make sure their police forces understand slavery and trafficking and are equipped to handle such cases.[50]

In fact, Bales and Cornell assert, in many countries corrupt police are bribed by human traffickers to ignore the slave trade. In India, for example, Bales and Cornell allege that many police officers are willing to take bribes to ignore cases of debt bondage or trafficking in prostitutes. "Police corruption is one of the biggest obstacles to reducing slavery in India,"[51] they say.

Corrupt and Despotic

Most law enforcement agencies that do look into cases of slavery focus on prostitution, uncovering evidence of human trafficking as they investigate sex-for-pay rings. The FBI established the Human Trafficking Initiative in 2005, lending its investigative resources to local police departments that probe prostitution rings they believe are using girls who have been kidnapped from their home countries and made to work in the sex business. In Southern California the Los Angeles Metro Task Force on Human Trafficking uses agents from the FBI as well as the Los Angeles Police Department, US Immigration and Customs Enforcement, the US Labor Department, and the Offices of the US Attorneys.

Where Are the Most Slaves?

The Australian-based human rights group Walk Free Foundation issues an annual report identifying the countries where slavery is most prevalent. In the group's 2013 report, the African nation of Mauritania was identified as the country with the highest percentage of enslaved people relative to the population. The Walk Free Foundation found that 160,000 people, or 4.2 percent of the country's 3.8 million citizens, are slaves.

The country with the most slaves is India, with as many as 15 million people serving in some form of slavery, according to the Walk Free Foundation. India has an overall population of 1.2 billion people, meaning just over 1 percent of the population serves in slavery.

Mauritania is known for its system of descent-based slavery, where people in the lower castes are forced to serve as slaves for the wealthy. In India most of enslaved people serve in bonded slavery or in the sex trade.

The United States is believed to have about sixty-three thousand people who can be considered slaves. Most are the victims of human trafficking and work as prostitutes.

In 2010 the Los Angeles Metro Task Force announced the convictions of nine defendants, members of the Vasquez-Valenzuela crime family. They had been charged with kidnapping several young girls from their villages in Guatemala and illegally smuggling them into California, where they were forced to work as prostitutes. Said a statement issued by Immigration and Customs Enforcement:

The defendants intimidated and controlled their victims by threatening to beat them and kill their loved ones in Guatemala if they tried to escape. Some defendants also used witch doctors to threaten the girls that a curse would be placed on them and their families. At least two of the defendants further restrained the victims by locking them in at night and blocking windows and doors. The defendants also used verbal abuse and psychological manipulation and control to reinforce their control over the victims. The defendants imposed strict controls over the victims' work schedules and made ominous comments about consequences that befell the families of other victims who attempted to escape.[52]

Following their convictions, the nine defendants were sentenced to prison terms as long as forty years. Clearly, the cases brought against the Vasquez-Valenzuela family illustrate that slavery is taken very seriously in American society and that those who are convicted in human trafficking cases face lengthy prison sentences. That is not necessarily true in other countries. In India police are willing to take bribes to ignore human trafficking and debt bondage, while in Uzbekistan members of the military serve as willing conspirators in the government's long-standing policy of enslaving people to work in the cotton fields, where they help enrich the coffers of what is obviously a corrupt and despotic administration. Despite the resolve of the United Nations as well as individual countries to stamp out slavery, the enslavement of people remains an element of human civilization in the twenty-first century.

Chapter 5

What Is the Legacy of Slavery?

Two centuries after outlawing the slave trade, eight European nations are facing demands for apologies and reparations by descendants of the peoples they once enslaved. In 2013 fourteen Caribbean countries announced plans to compile a report chronicling the economic and social damages committed against them during the centuries in which their citizens were forced to work as slaves. When the report is completed, the Caribbean countries plan to press the European nations for monetary payments to compensate them for their suffering. The European countries targeted for reparations are Great Britain, France, Netherlands, Spain, Portugal, Denmark, Norway, and Sweden.

In fact, leaders of the Caribbean countries point to the widespread poverty in their nations and insist their economies are still suffering because of slavery. During the era of the slave trade, they argue, slaves had no opportunities to own land or businesses and accumulate wealth. After the slaves were freed, they were left largely on their own. Over the past two centuries, their descendants have been mired in the same poverty in which their ancestors found themselves after gaining their freedom from bondage. Baldwin Spencer, prime minister of the Caribbean nation of Antigua and Barbuda, argues, "Our constant search for development resources is linked directly to the historical inability of our nations to accumulate wealth from the efforts of our peoples during slavery and colonialism."[53]

The case for reparations the Caribbean nations intend to make illustrates that centuries after the end of slavery, the effects of the enslavement of people continue to haunt their descendants. Many have been mired in poverty because the enslavement of their ancestors provided them no firm ground on which to build families, accumulate wealth, or make life better for themselves or their descendants.

Widespread Poverty

Following completion of the report, the Caribbean nations plan to present their case to the International Court of Justice (ICJ) at The Hague. The court in Netherlands was established to preside over international disputes and in the past has ordered countries to pay reparations to victims of war crimes. Martyn Day, a British attorney retained by the Caribbean nations to compile the report, insisted that the countries, representing the descendants of former slaves, will present a case the court would accept. "What happened in the Caribbean and West Africa was

Corrugated boards form the walls of houses in a poor neighborhood on Antigua. Poverty is one legacy of slavery on this Caribbean island nation.

so egregious we feel that bringing a case in the ICJ would have a decent chance of success," he said. "The fact that you were subjugating a whole class of people in a massively discriminatory way has no parallel."[54]

The issue of paying reparations to the descendants of slaves has also been raised in the US Congress. As far back as 1989, Michigan representative John Conyers introduced legislation to study the issue of making reparations for slavery to African Americans, but the bill has been stalled in committee. Clearly, Congress is balking at the prospect of paying reparations that could likely total in the hundreds of millions of dollars to African Americans who can prove they are the descendants of slaves.

Proponents of paying reparations to the descendants of slaves point to the widespread poverty suffered by many African Americans. They argue that their circumstances can be traced back to the enslavement of their ancestors.

The impact of the end of slavery on American society started soon after the Civil War. Many citizens in the southern states refused to accept the former slaves as equals. Indeed, for decades after the Civil War, the newly freed slaves and their descendants bore the brunt of southern hatred and discrimination. Although they were granted full citizenship under the Thirteenth, Fourteenth, and Fifteenth Amendments to the US Constitution, the former slaves were terrorized by white southerners. The original Ku Klux Klan, established in the late 1860s by Confederate army veterans, terrorized blacks, often lynching them. In later years southern states passed the so-called Jim Crow laws, designed to rob blacks of their civil rights and ensure segregation in all aspects of southern society, including schools and public transportation.

The Jim Crow laws gave birth to a civil rights movement that finally achieved its aims in the 1950s and 1960s as leaders organized demonstrations against discrimination, won Supreme Court decisions outlawing segregation, and convinced Congress to pass a series of laws designed to ensure voting rights and desegregation of all American institutions. Still, although former slaves and their descendants have won citizenship and equal rights under federal law, the wounds of slavery—largely economic hardship for the African American community—have endured for generations.

Forty Acres and a Mule

Even 150 years after emancipation, many African Americans are mired in poverty—a circumstance many sociologists trace to the enslavement of their ancestors. According to the Kaiser Family Foundation, which studies social issues in American society, 35 percent of African Americans live at or below the federal poverty line that is calculated by the US Department of Health and Human Services. The poverty line has been calculated at an annual income of $23,850 for a family of four. In contrast, the Kaiser Family Foundation found that 33 percent of Latinos and 13 percent of whites live below the poverty line.

Economic conditions are harshest for African Americans living in the former slaveholding states. In Mississippi and Louisiana, for example, the Kaiser Family Foundation found that 44 percent of African American families live below the federal poverty line. In Arkansas 48 percent of African Americans—virtually half the African American population of the state—live below the federal poverty line.

Sociologists point out that household wealth is largely accumulated over several generations—parents leave their children their assets; those assets grow from generation to generation. After emancipation, though, slaves found themselves with few pennies in their pockets and, due to the racism in the South, few opportunities to obtain jobs that would pay them enough to accumulate wealth. University of Wisconsin sociologist Heather A. O'Connell states, "Slavery officially ended 150 years ago. However, despite its dissolution, it has shaped social, economic and political agendas since its inception in the United States."[55]

As the Civil War drew to a close, Union leaders were well aware they could not leave the former slaves without opportunities to fend for themselves. In January 1865, when it had become clear to Union leaders that the Confederacy would fall, Union general William Tecumseh Sherman and Secretary of War Edwin M. Stanton devised a plan to seize hundreds of thousands of acres of land from plantation owners in South Carolina, Georgia, and Florida. Sherman and Stanton proposed to resettle the former slaves on these lands. Under the plan, each former slave would receive 40 acres (16.2 ha) to farm. Moreover, under the order signed by Sherman, the US Army would maintain a force of

Freed slaves (pictured) endured hatred and discrimination in the South despite their newly won status as US citizens. They suffered at the hands of groups such as the Ku Klux Klan and under laws passed by southern legislators.

soldiers in the region to ensure protection for the former slaves. "By the laws of war," the order read, "and orders of the President of the United States, the negro is free and must be dealt with as such."[56] At some point after Sherman signed the order, according to folklore, a mule was also promised to each of the former slaves—hence, the saying that the former slaves were promised "forty acres and a mule."

Oppressive Poverty

When Sherman and Stanton conceived the plan, the war was not yet over—Southern commander General Robert E. Lee did not surrender to

Union general Ulysses S. Grant until April 9, 1865. In the Deep South, however, the war had all but ended following Sherman's march through Georgia in November and December of the previous year. Therefore, soon after Sherman signed the order granting land to the free slaves, thousands flocked to Georgia to claim their farmsteads. In Chatham County, Georgia, one thousand freed slaves established their own community and elected a minister, Ulysses L. Houston, as their governor.

A few months later, all would be evicted. After the assassination of Abraham Lincoln on April 14, 1865, the vice president, Andrew Johnson, ascended to the presidency. Johnson caved in to pressure by southern politicians to return the land to the plantation owners. Johnson was made to believe southerners would be more willing to accept Reconstruction if they got their land back. The land was returned to the plantation owners, and the emancipated slaves were forced to enter American society with no money in their pockets, no land to farm, and few opportunities to break out of the oppressive poverty that awaited them and their descendants.

Paying for Past Wrongdoings

Even after all these years, activists believe African Americans should press their case, pointing out that Germany set up a $60 billion fund to pay Jewish survivors of Nazi war crimes, including those who were forced to work as slaves in munitions factories. Moreover, in 1999 Congress completed payments of $1.6 billion to 120,000 Japanese Americans who were wrongfully interned in camps during World War II because they were suspected of being saboteurs, spies, and rebels who could have assisted the Japanese during the war. Therefore, proponents of reparations for African Americans point out there is precedence for paying those who were ill treated by history. Elazar Barkan, chair of cultural studies at Claremont University in California, claims, "For better or worse [we] should pay our historical debts."[57]

Meanwhile, other groups continue to press for reparations. In 1993 the Japanese government issued a formal apology for the enslavement of the comfort women during World War II but resisted

Charles Darwin and Slavery

The science of evolution can largely be attributed to one man's abhorrence of slavery and his commitment to prove that the slaves captured in Africa were deserving of human rights and, therefore, freedom. In 1831 naturalist Charles Darwin began a voyage aboard the HMS *Beagle*. Darwin traveled virtually around the world, stopping in ports where he observed conditions under which slaves were forced to live. While visiting Brazil, Darwin wrote, "To this day, if I hear a distant scream, it recalls with painful vividness my feelings . . . that some poor slave was being tortured."

During this era there was a pervading attitude among slave owners that slaves were not actually human—they were members of a species more akin to beasts of burden. Write Darwin's biographers Adrian Desmond and James Moore, "Slavery, justified by the planters' belief that black slaves were a separately created animal species, was the immoral blot on [Darwin's] youthful landscape and a spur to his emancipist study of the origins—evolution, we call it today."

In 1871 Darwin published *The Descent of Man*, in which he proposed that all people are members of a single race—the human race. He wrote, "All the races agree in so many unimportant details of structure and in so many mental peculiarities, that these can be accounted for only through inheritance from a common progenitor; and a progenitor thus characterized would probably have deserved the rank of man."

Quoted in Christopher Benfey, "Charles Darwin, Abolitionist," *New York Times*, February 1, 2009, p. BR11.

Adrian Desmond and James Moore, *Darwin's Sacred Cause: How a Hatred of Slavery Shaped Darwin's Views on Human Evolution*. Boston: Houghton Mifflin Harcourt, 2009, p. 1.

Quoted in Desmond and Moore, *Darwin's Sacred Cause*, p. 367.

calls to pay reparations. Former slaves have filed lawsuits in Japanese courts seeking reparations, but the courts have refused to order compensation paid to them.

Despite the refusal of Japanese courts to award damages, former comfort women and their supporters have vowed to keep up the pressure on the Japanese government. Throughout Asia surviving comfort women—all of them now elderly—often attend protests outside the gates of Japanese embassies. In Seoul, South Korea, a protest is held in front of the Japanese embassy every Wednesday. A handful of former comfort women—most of them in their eighties—attend the demonstrations along with young people who march with them in support. One former Korean brothel worker, eighty-seven-year-old Kim Bok-dong, asserts, "I came here to ask Japan to settle its past wrongdoing. I hope the Japanese government resolves the problem as soon as possible while we elderly women are still alive."[58]

Lack of Population Growth

As the former comfort women as well as descendants of slaves press their cases for reparations, leaders of countries where slaves were captured believe there is no way to make up for the damage caused to their societies by the slave traders. As in the United States and the Caribbean states, the African countries where slaves were captured and sold also believe they have been mired in poverty largely because of the slave trade. Historians believe there is no accurate way to tell how many Africans were forced into slavery since the earliest years of the slave trade in the ancient era. Some historians believe as many as 100 million Africans may have been displaced during centuries of slave trading.

Today Africa is regarded as a sparsely populated continent. According to one scholar, the late Guyanese historian Walter Rodney, the population of Africa grew little during the height of the slave trade—from 100 million in 1650 to 120 million in 1900. In contrast, during that same period the population of Europe grew from 103 million to 423 million, and the population of Asia grew from 257 million to 857 million. The lack of population growth in the continent has had a wide-ranging impact on the African people. Festus Ugboajo Ohaegbulam, a professor of international relations at the University of South Florida, writes:

> The slave trade robbed Africa . . . through the uprooting of its surviving victims, incalculable millions of people who were among the most virile and active members of its population. This means that Africa lost a great deal of its productive as well as reproductive capacity as it remained underpopulated for the centuries of the slave trade. The negative impact of this consequence of the [slave] trade on the economic development processes in Africa was far-reaching. Under-population of Africa during the [slave] trade ensured that the ratio of population to land remained very low; that population remained largely dispersed, forests untamed, cultivation extensive rather than intensive; and that local self-sufficiency remained the rule. . . . Agriculture, for the most part, remained uncommercialized.[59]

Polygamy and Political Turmoil

Moreover, Ohaegbulam points out, most of the slaves who were captured and sent to other countries were males. As such, their loss in African communities affected the social dynamics of life in Africa. A shortage of males ensured the continuation of polygamy well into the modern era—polygamy is still found in Sudan and Senegal.

Ohaegbulam also believes the instability of African communities caused by the sudden loss of adult men has been a contributing factor to the political turmoil that has plagued many African countries into the twenty-first century. As Africans have been forced to endure dictators, revolutions, civil wars, and other disruptions to their societies, countries on other continents have achieved advances in technology and industrialization. Says Ohaegbulam:

> The overseas slave trade created so much chaos and so undermined elements of civilization in Africa that Europeans who traversed tropical Africa in the nineteenth century imagined that chaos and

Displaced women and children from Sudan await help in a refugee camp. The instability caused by so many African men being taken as slaves has contributed to ongoing political turmoil in many African countries.

desolation were historically endemic to Africa. When Africa woke up from the consequences of the [slave] trade, it found that other members of humanity, especially in the Western European world, had reached a much higher standard of technological change which further facilitated their exploitation of Africa.[60]

Their Masters' Names

Those slaves who were captured in Africa and shipped to America and other countries lost more than their freedom—they lost their identities. Today most African Americans do not know their true family names— the surnames they use today were given to their ancestors as they arrived in America, and frequently those names were the names of their masters. Sometimes they were given names based on their duties—a slave trained as a blacksmith may have been given the surname Smith by his owner or a local census taker. Slaves who were sold to new masters often found themselves forced to accept new last names. That is what happened to the slaves owned by Nathaniel Terry, a Kentucky plantation owner. After Terry's death, his fifty slaves—all of whom used the surname Terry— were sold to other plantations, where they were told they would now use the surnames of their new masters. Following emancipation most of those slaves chose to return to using the surname Terry because it was the name that had been used by their fathers, mothers, grandparents, and other relatives. "Their families had been with the white Terry family for generations,"[61] says genealogist and author John F. Baker Jr.

After emancipation, many former slaves adopted the surnames of American presidents and other historical figures they admired. Genealogists and historians acknowledge that it is difficult for most African Americans to learn their true family names—or even much about their African ancestors—because in the slave-trading era, record keeping of births, deaths, and other family milestones was rare and, in fact, virtually unheard of in Africa.

DNA Testing

In recent years many African Americans have turned to DNA testing to help trace their roots. Some universities as well as private companies collect tissue samples from clients—usually drawn from the insides of their cheeks. Through DNA analyses, researchers attempt to match clients with the tribes of their ancestors or at least the regions of Africa where their ancestors were likely to have been born. DNA is composed of genetic material in which common traits—such as hair and eye color and even diseases—are passed down from generation to generation.

Researchers believe this process is in its infancy because the DNA database of African ancestry is very small. At the University of Chicago, geneticist Rick Kittles has traveled to Africa several times since the 1990s, collecting DNA samples from members of African ethnic groups

Communism's Roots in Slavery

A significant legacy of slavery on the people of Europe first surfaced in the London flat of the German-born writer Karl Marx. In 1848 Marx and coauthor Friedrich Engels wrote *The Communist Manifesto*, which established the principles on which the international Communist movement was based. During this era, there was no middle class—a few people were very wealthy but most were poor, working on farms, as craftspeople, or for low wages in the dismal factories of the Industrial Revolution. Marx envisioned a day when the workers would throw off the chains of economic oppression and end the class system.

Thirteen years after publishing *The Communist Manifesto*, Marx came across the story of Spartacus and found much inspiration in the tale of the Roman slaves who rose up against their masters. In a letter to Engels, Marx wrote, "Spartacus appears to be the most capital fellow that all of ancient history can show for itself. Great general, a noble character, real representative of the ancient [worker]."

As the Communist movement spread across Europe, other leftist leaders found inspiration in the story of Spartacus. In post–World War I Germany, a Communist movement that called itself the Spartacists attempted to seize power. The Spartacists, led by Karl Liebknecht and Rosa Luxemburg, attempted their coup in January 1919. The German army remained loyal to the shaky democratic government and violently put down the Spartacist uprising. Liebknecht and Luxemburg were captured and executed by army officers. In subsequent years the fear in Germany of a Communist takeover of the government helped the Nazi Party come to power, and along with it, the determination of Adolf Hitler to conquer Europe.

Quoted in Martin M. Winkler, *Spartacus: Film and History*. Malden, MA: Blackwell, 2007, p. 2.

in some thirty countries. Kittles has amassed a collection of more than twelve thousand DNA samples. By having their DNA matched with the samples in Kittles's collection or in the collections of other researchers, African Americans can often identify the countries or tribes of origin of their ancestors who were captured and sold into slavery.

But since the DNA database is still relatively small, it could be difficult for researchers to pinpoint the ancestries of their clients. For example, the American astronaut Mae Jemison provided a DNA sample to learn her roots. The test showed only that her ancestors were likely to have been born in a region somewhere from Senegal to Gabon—a huge swath of African territory covering some 2.4 million square miles (6.2 million sq. km). Another geneticist, Bruce A. Jackson of the University of Massachusetts, says it may take at least another generation of DNA collection before geneticists can provide African Americans with clearer pictures of who their ancestors were. "It's that daunting a job,"[62] he says.

Still Part of Human Culture

As DNA science progresses, it is possible that more and more African Americans will learn new truths about their origins. Still, it is likely the legacies of slavery will continue for generations. In the Caribbean nations the descendants of former slaves are expected to press for reparations in international courts in a process that could take years to resolve. And even if they do win reparations from the countries that made their ancestors into slaves, a troubling fact about slavery remains: Around the globe an estimated 21 million people continue to serve in some form of slavery. They may be forced to pick cotton by the dictatorial government of Uzbekistan, kidnapped by human traffickers and forced into prostitution, or made to serve their masters because they live in societies that regard them as members of lower castes. However they are forced to serve, the fact remains that since before the days of Spartacus, humans have sought to enslave other humans. Well into the twenty-first century, democratic governments, human rights activists, and rebellious slaves themselves have been unable to find ways to eliminate slavery from human culture.

Source Notes

Introduction: The Defining Characteristics of Slavery

1. Jeremy Black, *Slavery: A New Global History*. London: Running Press, 2011, p. 2.

Chapter One: What Conditions Led to Slavery?

2. Milton Meltzer, *Slavery: A World History*, vol. 1. Cambridge, MA: Da Capo, 1993, p. 1.
3. J.A.K. Thomson, trans., *The Ethics of Aristotle*. Middlesex, England: Penguin Classics, 1973, p. 249.
4. Meltzer, *Slavery*, vol. 1, p. 75.
5. Meltzer, *Slavery*, vol. 1, p. 59.
6. Sara Forsdyke, *Slaves Tell Tales: And Other Episodes in the Politics of Popular Culture in Ancient Greece*. Princeton, NJ: Princeton University Press, 2012, p. 86.
7. Meltzer, *Slavery*, vol. 1, p. 79.
8. Meltzer, *Slavery*, vol. 1, p. 58.
9. Meltzer, *Slavery*, vol. 1, p. 79.
10. Robert Osborne, *Greek History*. London: Routledge, 2004, p. 94.
11. Meltzer, *Slavery*, vol. 1, p. 113.
12. Quoted in Will Durant, *Caesar and Christ: The Story of Civilization*, vol. 3. New York: Simon & Schuster, 1944, p. 137.
13. Durant, *Caesar and Christ*, p. 138.

Chapter Two: Slaves of the Medieval Era

14. Ruth A. Johnston, *All Things Medieval: An Encyclopedia of the Medieval World*. Santa Barbara, CA: Greenwood, 2011, p. 639.
15. Quoted in Meltzer, *Slavery*, vol. 1, p. 213.
16. Quoted in Junius P. Rodriguez, ed., *The Historical Encyclopedia of World Slavery*, vol. 1. Santa Barbara, CA: ABC-CLIO, 1997, p. 99.
17. Quoted in Carole Hillenbrande, *The Crusades: Islamic Perspectives*. New York: Routledge, 2000, p. 550.
18. Yvonne Friedman, *Encounters Between Enemies: Captivity and Ransom in the Latin Kingdom of Jerusalem*. Leiden, Netherlands: Brill, 2002, p. 44.
19. Quoted in Rodriguez, *The Historical Encyclopedia of World Slavery*, vol. 1, pp. 261–62.
20. Will Durant, *The Age of Faith: The Story of Civilization*, vol. 4. New York: Simon & Schuster, 1950, p. 554.

21. Black, *Slavery*, p. 4.

22. Black, *Slavery*, pp. 38–39.

23. Durant, *The Age of Faith*, p. 557.

24. Meltzer, *Slavery*, vol. 1, p. 228.

25. Quoted in Will Durant, *The Reformation: The Story of Civilization*, vol. 6. New York: Simon & Schuster, 1957, p. 44.

26. Quoted in Durant, *The Reformation*, p. 45.

27. Durant, *The Reformation*, p. 45.

28. Michael Wood, *The Great Turning Point of British History: The 20 Events That Made the Nation*. London: Constable, 2013, eBook.

29. John Kellis Ingram, *A History of Slavery and Serfdom*. London: Adam and Charles Black, 1895, p. 104.

Chapter Three: Slavery in the New World

30. James Horn, *A Land as God Make It: Jamestown and the Birth of America*. New York: Basic Books, 2006, p. 287.

31. Meltzer, *Slavery: A World History*, vol. 2. Cambridge, MA: Da Capo, 1993, p. 128.

32. Quoted in Gordon S. Wood., *The Americanization of Benjamin Franklin*. New York: Penguin, 2002, p. 228.

33. Quoted in Wood, *The Americanization of Benjamin Franklin*, p. 229.

34. Gavin Weightman, *The Industrial Revolutionaries: The Making of the Modern World, 1776–1914*. New York: Grove, 2007, pp. 107–108.

35. Meltzer, *Slavery*, vol. 2, p. 158.

36. Meltzer, *Slavery*, vol. 2, pp. 211–12.

37. Quoted in Meltzer, *Slavery*, vol. 2, p. 164.

38. Quoted in Meltzer, *Slavery*, vol. 2, p. 239.

Chapter Four: Slavery in the Modern Era

39. Nike Inc., "Statement on Uzbekistan Cotton Production," December 8, 2009. http://nikeinc.com.

40. Quoted in Mansur Mirovalev and Andrew E. Kramer, "In Uzbekistan, the Practice of Forced Labor Lives On During the Cotton Harvest," *New York Times*, December 18, 2013, p. A-10.

41. Quoted in Ethical Trading Initiative, "Joanna Ewart-James," July 17, 2012. www.ethicaltrade.org.

42. Quoted in Seth Mydans, "Inside a Wartime Brothel: The Avenger's Story," *New York Times*, November 12, 1996, p. A-4.

43. Quoted in Andrew Cockburn, "21st Century Slaves," *National Geographic*, September 2003, p. 8.

44. Quoted in Anti-Slavery International, "What Is Modern Slavery?," 2014. www.antislavery.org.

45. Ericka Anderson, "Morning Bell: The UN's Terrible Record on Human Rights," *The Foundry* (blog), Heritage Foundation, June 28, 2011. http://blog.heritage.org.

46. Kevin Bales and Becky Cornell, *Slavery Today*. Toronto: Groundwood, 2008, p. 7.

47. Susan Tiefenbrun, "Child Soldiers, Slavery and the Trafficking of Children," *Fordham International Law Journal*, 2007, pp. 417–18.

48. Anti-Slavery International, "Bonded Labour," 2014. www.antislavery.org.

49. Quoted in Steve Hargreaves, "I Was a Modern-Day Slave in America," CNN, November 25, 2013. http://money.cnn.com.

50. Bales and Cornell, *Slavery Today*, p. 103.

51. Bales and Cornell, *Slavery Today*, p. 72.

52. US Immigration and Customs Enforcement, "Five Defendants Convicted of Sex Trafficking for Forcing Guatemalan Girls and Women into Prostitution," February 11, 2009. www.ice.gov.

Chapter Five: What Is the Legacy of Slavery?

53. Quoted in Stephen Castle, "Caribbean Nations to Seek Reparations, Putting Price on Damage of Slavery," *New York Times*, October 21, 2013, p. A-4.

54. Quoted in Castle, "Caribbean Nations to Seek Reparations, Putting Price on Damage of Slavery," p. A-4.

55. Heather A. O'Connell, "The Impact of Slavery on Racial Equality in Poverty in the Contemporary US South," *Social Forces*, March 2012, pp. 715–16.

56. Quoted in Henry Louis Gates Jr., "The Truth Behind '40 Acres and a Mule,'" *The African Americans: Many Rivers to Cross*, PBS, 2013. www.pbs.org.

57. Quoted in Diane Cardwell, "Seeking Out a Just Way to Make Amends for Slavery," *New York Times*, August 12, 2000, p. B7.

58. Quoted in *New Zealand Herald* (Auckland, New Zealand), "Anguish from Japan's Sex Slave Legacy Unsettled," May 29, 2013.

59. Festus Ugboajo Ohaegbulam, *Towards an Understanding of the African Experience from Historical and Contemporary Perspectives*. Lanham, MD: University Press of America, 1990, p. 148.

60. Ohaegbulam, *Towards an Understanding of the African Experience from Historical and Contemporary Perspectives*, p. 148.

61. John F. Baker Jr., "Surnames Used by African American Slaves," *The Washingtons of Wessyngton Plantation* (blog), August 28, 2009. www.wessyngton.com.

62. Quoted in Toni Coleman, "Regaining a Lost Heritage," *Issues in Higher Education*, February 8, 2007, p. 28.

Important People in the History of Slavery

Simón Bolívar: The wealthy member of a slaveholding family, Bolívar was nevertheless a staunch abolitionist. In the early 1800s he led revolutions to free Ecuador, Colombia, Venezuela, Peru, and Bolivia from Spanish rule. After winning their independence from Spain, all those nations outlawed slavery.

John Brown: While other abolitionists sought peaceful efforts to outlaw slavery in America, Brown was convinced armed insurrection was the only course that would work. In 1859 he staged a raid on a US military armory in Harpers Ferry, Virginia. The raid was put down by US Army troops; Brown was arrested and hanged for treason.

Charles Darwin: The British naturalist's hatred for slavery influenced his work in developing the science of evolution. In 1871 Darwin published the book *The Descent of Man* in which he declared that humans of all races are descended from the same ancestors.

Drimachus: The sixth-century-BCE Greek slave became a godlike figure to other slaves after he staged a revolt on the island of Chios. Greek soldiers failed in their many efforts to flush Drimachus out of his mountain hideaway, from where he staged raids against slaveholders, freeing their slaves and punishing cruel taskmasters.

Elizabeth I: Queen Elizabeth I freed the English serfs in 1574 but helped spark the slave trade in the New World when she used her personal wealth to finance a 1564 voyage by the admiral John Hawkins, who captured slaves in the African country of Sierra Leone and sold them in Venezuela.

Benjamin Franklin: The Philadelphia printer, inventor, and statesman rose to become one of America's earliest and most influential abolitionists, attaining the presidency of the Society for Promoting the Abolition of Slavery and the Relief of Negroes Unlawfully Held in Bondage. Franklin's group failed to convince Congress to outlaw slavery but helped establish abolitionism as a movement that would continue to grow and become influential in American politics.

John Hawkins: In 1562 Hawkins, a British navy admiral, realized huge profits when he started trading slaves he captured in Africa to plantation owners in the Caribbean islands. Hawkins became the most successful slave trader in the mid-sixteenth century, helping to establish a robust commerce in African slaves in the New World. His ventures were financed by Queen Elizabeth I.

Islam Karimov: The despotic president of Uzbekistan orders his country's military to round up citizens each year to pick cotton for little or no pay. The workers, many of whom are children, are forced to live in squalid barracks near the cotton fields. Workers who refuse are fired from their jobs, jailed, and often tortured.

Abraham Lincoln: The sixteenth US president opposed expansion of slavery into the American territories, a position the southern states found intolerable. His election in 1860 touched off secession and the ensuing American Civil War. In 1863 Lincoln issued the Emancipation Proclamation, freeing all American slaves held in territories that were in rebellion against the Union.

Pasion: The fourth-century-BCE Roman slave was placed in charge of his owners' bank. Pasion proved so valuable to the business that he was granted his freedom and eventually given ownership of the bank. Pasion became so wealthy that he was able to buy his own slaves.

Dred Scott: Scott was a black slave born in Virginia who later moved to Missouri, where he was sold to another master. When that individual took Scott to two nonslave states (Illinois and Wisconsin) to live briefly before returning to Missouri, Scott launched a suit in the Missouri courts, claiming he was free because he had lived in territories that prohibited slavery. In 1857 the US Supreme Court ruled against Scott, finding that slaves were not American citizens and therefore entitled to no rights under the US Constitiution.

Saladin: The powerful sultan defeated a Christian army at the Battle of Hattin in 1187 in what is today the modern state of Israel. Saladin's army captured most of the twenty thousand Christian soldiers and sold them into slavery. So many Christians were turned into slaves that traders complained the abundance of slaves had driven down the price to the point that a slave could be bought at auction for a pair of sandals.

Spartacus: Born in Thrace, Spartacus was taken captive by the Romans and trained as a gladiator. After making his escape Spartacus raised an army of 120,000 slaves, which he hoped to lead to freedom. The uprising, known as the Third Servile War, ended in 71 BCE when the slave army was defeated by Roman soldiers at the Battle of Siler River. Spartacus died in the battle, and the surviving slaves were crucified.

Wat Tyler: The leader of the Peasants' Revolt of 1381, which attempted to win freedom for English serfs, Tyler was killed by a bodyguard of King Richard II during a meeting to resolve the peasants' grievances. Witnessing the murder, Tyler's supporters raised their bows, but Richard stepped forward and promised to agree to all their demands as a ploy to buy time. Shortly after the incident, Richard reneged on his promises and had the leaders arrested and executed.

Eli Whitney: In 1793 the Massachusetts scholar invented a device to "gin" cotton—to mechanically eliminate the seeds from cotton fibers—making it easy to turn the fibers into fabrics. Whitney's invention established the South as the cotton capital of the world and created an enormous need for slaves to pick cotton.

Books

Jeremy Black, *Slavery: A New Global History*. London: Running Press, 2011.

Keith Bradley, ed., *The Cambridge World History of Slavery: Volume 2, AD 500–AD 1420*. Cambridge: Cambridge University Press, 2012.

Keith Bradley and Paul Cartledge, eds., *The Cambridge World History of Slavery: Volume 1, The Ancient Mediterranean World*. Cambridge: Cambridge University Press, 2011.

David Eltis and Stanley L. Engerman, eds., *The Cambridge World History of Slavery: Volume 3, AD 1420–AD 1804*. Cambridge: Cambridge University Press, 2011.

Sara Forsdyke, *Slaves Tell Tales: And Other Episodes in the Politics of Popular Culture in Ancient Greece*. Princeton, NJ: Princeton University Press, 2012.

Greg Grandin, *The Empire of Necessity: Slavery, Freedom, and Deception in the New World*. New York: Metropolitan, 2014.

Stephanie Hepburn and Rita J. Simon, *Human Trafficking Around the World: Hidden in Plain Sight*. New York: Columbia University Press, 2013.

Jenny S. Martinez, *The Slave Trade and the Origins of International Human Rights*. Oxford: Oxford University Press, 2014.

Solomon Northup and Sue Eakin, *12 Years a Slave*. Longboat Key, FL: Telemachus, 2013.

Peipei Qiu, Su Zhiliang, and Chen Lifei, *Chinese Comfort Women: Testimonies from Imperial Japan's Sex Slaves.* Vancouver: University of British Columbia Press, 2013.

Aldo Schiavone, *Spartacus.* Cambridge, MA: Harvard University Press, 2013.

Websites

Africans in America (www.pbs.org/wgbh/aia/home.html). Companion website to the 1998 PBS documentary *Africans in America.* Visitors can find a narrative covering the entire history of slavery in America. Among the features available on the website are a timeline of events in American slavery and interactive maps that identify key developments in the institution of slavery with the places where they happened, such as John Brown's raid on Harpers Ferry, Virginia.

Anti-Slavery International (www.antislavery.org). The London-based human rights group tracks slavery in twenty-first-century society and advocates for the release of slaves and government reforms to abolish slavery. By following the link for "Slavery Today," visitors can find explanations and current examples of human trafficking, bonded slavery, forced labor, and child slavery.

John Brown's Harpers Ferry Raid (www.civilwar.org/150th-anniversary/john-browns-harpers-ferry.html). The website, maintained by the historical group Civil War Trust, provides a narrative on the raid staged by the radical Abolitionist John Brown on the US military armory at Harpers Ferry, Virginia. Visitors can find maps, featuring Brown's route to Harpers Ferry; a chronology of the events before and after the raid, and biographies of Brown as well as army commanders J.E.B. Stuart and Robert E. Lee, who defeated Brown at Harpers Ferry.

7 Famous Slave Revolts (www.history.com/news/history-lists/7-famous-slave-revolts). Maintained by the History Channel, the website chronicles seven slave uprisings, including the Third Servile War led by Spartacus, the 1801 uprising of the slaves in Haiti, and the 1831 uprising in Virginia led by the slave Nat Turner in which more than fifty slaveholders were killed. Visitors can find illustrations and narratives of the events.

Slavery: A 21st Century Evil (www.aljazeera.com/programmes/slavery a21stcenturyevil). The TV network Al Jazeera produced a four-part series in 2011 focusing on slavery in the twenty-first century. Visitors to the companion website can learn about consumer goods made with slave labor that are sold in America and other democratic countries, how human sex traffickers snare young women into prostitution, and how Brazilians are lured into remote jungle camps where they are made into slaves to produce charcoal.

Slavery and Empire (www.bbc.co.uk/programmes/p00548jd). This is a companion website to 2002 documentary produced by BBC Radio on the English slave trade. Visitors can listen to an archived broadcast of the documentary and also find a text narrative and illustrations of English slave traders.

Slavery in the 21st Century (www.npr.org/templates/story/story.php ?storyId=1408233). This is the companion website to the 2003 National Public Radio broadcast in which the issue of modern-day slavery is examined by the network's correspondents. Visitors can hear an archived broadcast of the show, view photographs of modern-day slaves, and find links to feature stories published in *National Geographic* and *Scientific American* examining slavery in the twenty-first century.

US Department of State Office to Monitor and Combat Trafficking in Persons (www.state.gov/j/tip). The agency works with other governments to monitor human trafficking and develop international strategies to break up trafficking rings. Visitors to the website can find instructions on how to identify victims of human trafficking and how people can notify authorities if they suspect a trafficking ring is operating in their neighborhood. Also, victims can find instructions on how to seek help. The instructions are available in more than a dozen languages.

Washington Coalition for Comfort Women Issues (www.comfort -women.org). Established in 1992, the organization provides educational resources about the plight of the comfort women. Visitors can find a timeline of events leading up to the enslavement of the comfort women, photos of enslaved women, and news about demonstrations staged by surviving comfort women and their supporters to seek reparations from the Japanese government.

Index

Picture Credits

About the Author

Hal Marcovitz is a former newspaper reporter and columnist. He is the author of more than 150 books for young readers. His other titles in the Understanding World History series include *Rise of the Nazis*, *Ancient Rome*, *Ancient Greece*, *The Industrual Revolution*, and *The Arab Spring Uprising*.